plani'en u.

Istanbul

120th
anniversary
Berlitz

- A ☞ in the text denotes a highly recommended sight
- A complete A–Z of practical information starts on p.104
- Extensive mapping on cover flaps

Berlitz Publishing Company, Inc.
Princeton   Mexico City   Dublin   Eschborn   Singapore

Original Text:	Neil Wilson
Photography:	Neil Wilson
Editors:	Alan Tucker, Stephen Brewer
Layout:	Media Content Marketing, Inc.
Cartography:	GeoSystems Global Corporation

*Although we make every effort to ensure the accuracy of all infor-
mation in this book, changes do occur. If you find an error in this
guide, please let our editors know by writing to us at Berlitz Publishing Company, 400 Alexander Park, Princeton, NJ 08540-6306.
A postcard will do.*

ISBN 2-8315-6972-9
Revised 1998 – First Printing July 1998

Printed in Switzerland
019/807 REV

CONTENTS

Istanbul

THE CITY AND ITS PEOPLE

I stanbul is one of the world's most venerable cities. Part of the city's allure is its setting, where Europe faces Asia across the winding turquoise waters of the Bosphorus, making it the only city in the world to bridge two continents.

Here, where the waters of the Black Sea blend into the Aegean, East and West mingle and merge in the cultural melting-pot of Turkey's largest metropolis. Busy Oriental bazaars co-exist with European shops; kebab-shops and coffee-houses sit alongside international restaurants; modern office buildings and hotels alternate with Ottoman minarets along the city's skyline; traditional music and Western pop, belly-dancing and ballet, Turkish wrestling and football all compete for the attention of the *İstanbullu* audience.

This is the only city in the world to have been the capital of both an Islamic and a Christian empire. As Constantinople, jewel of the Byzantine Empire, it was for more than 1,000 years the most important city in Christendom. As Istanbul it was the seat of the Ottoman sultans, rulers of a 500-year Islamic empire that stretched from the Black Sea and the Balkans to Arabia and Algeria.

Istanbul owes its long-held historical significance to a strategic location at the mouth of the Bosphorus. From this vantage point the city could control not only the ships that passed through the strait on the important trade route between the Black Sea and the Mediterranean, but also the overland traffic travelling from Europe into Asia Minor, which used the narrow strait as a crossing point. In the words of the 16th-century French traveller Pierre Gilles: "The Bosphorus with one key opens and closes two worlds, two seas."

That strategic advantage is no less important today than it was 2,500 years ago, when a band of Greeks first founded the city of Byzantium on this very spot. Ankara may be the official capital of modern Turkey, but Istanbul remains the country's largest city, most important commercial centre, and busiest port, producing more than one-third of Turkey's manufacturing output. The Bosphorus is one of the world's most active shipping lanes, and the overland traffic is now carried by two of the world's longest suspension bridges.

The thriving city has long since spread beyond the fifth-century Byzantine walls built by the Emperor Theodosius II, and now sprawls for miles along the shores of the Sea of Marmara on both the European and Asian sides. Back in 1507 this was the world's largest city, with a population of 1.2 million. That figure has now passed 10 million and is still growing, swollen by a steady influx of people from rural areas looking for work (more than half the population was born in the provinces). These new arrivals have created a series of shanty-towns around the perimeter of the city. Their makeshift homes, known in Turkish as *gecekondu* ("built by night"), take advantage of an old Ottoman law that protects a house whose roof has been built during the hours of darkness. The slums are eventually knocked down to make way for new tower-blocks—a new suburb is created, yet another shanty-town springs beyond it, and Istanbul spreads out a little farther.

A mosaic detail from the ornate walls of Topkapı Palace.

At the other end of the social spectrum are the wealthy *İstanbullus,* who live in the upmarket districts of Taksim, Harbiye, and Nişantaşı, where the streets are lined with fashion boutiques, expensive apartments, and stylish cafés. Those belonging to this set are the lucky few who frequent the city's more expensive restaurants and casinos, and retire at the weekends to their restored wooden mansions (*yalı*) along the Bosphorus. But most of Istanbul's inhabitants fall between these two extremes, living in modest flats and earning an average wage in the offices, shops, banks, and factories that provide most of the city's employment.

Although small Armenian, Greek Orthodox, Jewish, and Catholic communities survive, the majority of *İstanbullus* are Muslim, and adhere to the principles known as the "Five Pillars of Islam"—to believe with all one's heart that "There is no God but God, and Mohammed is his Prophet"; to pray five times a day, at dawn, midday, afternoon, sunset, and after dark; to give alms to the poor, and towards the upkeep of the mosques; to fast between sunrise and sunset during the month of Ramadan; and to try to make the pilgrimage to Mecca at least once in one's lifetime. Those who have made the pilgrimage can add the respected title *haci* before their names, an honour proudly displayed on shop-owner's signs.

Just as the Bosphorus separates Asia from Europe, so the inlet called the Golden Horn separates the old Istanbul from the new. The main attractions for the visitor are concentrated in the historic heart of old Istanbul. Three great civilizations have shaped this part of the city—Roman, Byzantine, and Ottoman. Though little remains from Roman times, the city's Byzantine legacy boasts Haghia Sophia, the Church of the Divine Wisdom and one of the world's greatest buildings; the magnificent mosaics of St. Saviour in Chora; and the impressive Theodosian Walls. The Ottomans built count-

Local women happily model the traditional clothing of Turkey.

less mosques in their capital, the finest of which is the Süleymaniye, inspired by the form of the Haghia Sophia. But the most popular tourist sight is Topkapı Palace, the home of the Ottoman sultans, where the riches of the Imperial Treasury and the intrigue of the Harem draw many thousands of visitors each year.

From the *belvedere* in the treasury of the palace, where the Sultan used to gaze down upon his fleet, you can look across the mouth of the Golden Horn to the modern district of Beyoğlu, where multi-storey hotels rise beyond the turret of the Galata Tower. Down by the shore of the Bosphorus is the glittering façade of the 19th-century Dolmabahçe Palace, while beyond stretches the graceful span of the Bosphorus Bridge, a concrete symbol of the city, linking Europe with Asia.

Byzantium, Constantinople, Istanbul—down the centuries the city has been open to influences from both East and West, and this cross-fertilization of ideas has created one of the world's liveliest, most engaging, and most hospitable cultures. It is neither European nor Oriental, but an unparalleled and intoxicating blend; it is, quite simply, unique.

A BRIEF HISTORY

The modern Republic of Turkey dates only from 1923, but the history of the land within its borders stretches back to the dawn of humanity. Widespread finds of Stone Age implements in cave excavations show that Anatolia was already inhabited during the Middle of the Palaeolithic period (about 200,000 to 40,000 years ago). By Neolithic times, organized communities had arisen, such as the one at Çatalhöyük, near Konya, Turkey's most important prehistoric site. This town, which flourished between 6500 and 5500 B.C., had flat-roofed houses of mud and timber decorated with wall-paintings, some of which show patterns that still appear on Anatolian kilims.

The advent of the Bronze Age (about 3200 B.C.), and the spread of city-states ruled by kings, is marked by the appearance of royal tombs containing bronze objects in such places as Troy in the west, and Alacahöyük near Ankara. Around this time the Sumerian civilization living in Mesopotamia (the region between the Tigris and Euphrates rivers in present-day Iraq) founded and developed the cuneiform script, the world's oldest form of writing on record. The technique was introduced by Assyrian traders 1,000 years later into Anatolia, where it was quickly adopted by the indigenous Hatti people, who, at this point, had already reached an advanced state of civilization.

The Hittites

The capital of the Hatti was Kanesh (modern Kültepe, near Kayseri). Cuneiform tablets found here record the arrival in Anatolia of warlike invaders around the second millennium B.C. Their origins remain a mystery (their written language was finally deciphered in 1915), but they came from the direction of the Caucasus mountains, spreading destruction and disorder throughout Anatolia. It was two hundred years before they were firmly entrenched in their newly conquered empire.

The newcomers were the Hittites, and their domination of Anatolia can be divided into three distinct periods: the Old Kingdom (c. 1600–1450 B.C.), then the New or Empire Period (c. 1450–1200 B.C.), and the Late Hittite Period (c. 1200–700 B.C.). Their first capital city was Hattusa (now Boğazköy, near Ankara), which dates from the 13th century B.C. and has tombs, fortifications, enclosed temples, and a citadel containing an impressive library of more than 3,300 cuneiform tablets.

During the Empire Period, an ambitious Hittite king, Mutawallis, defeated the forces of the Egyptian pharaoh, Ramses II, at Kadesh (Syria) in 1285 B.C. Ramses was too proud to accept defeat, commissioning obelisks that celebrated his "victory." But he was sufficiently wary of the formidable strength of the Hittite Empire to make peace with the next king, Hattusili III. The Treaty of Kadesh, recorded on clay tablets on display in the Museum of the Ancient Orient in Istanbul (see page 39), is the oldest known example of an international treaty.

The Hittite Empire eventually collapsed following invasion from the west by the Achaeans, the Phrygians, and a mysterious force known only as the "Sea People." The Hittites were forced to flee south into the mountains, where they remained until they were absorbed by the Assyrians.

Troy and the Greeks

While the Hittite Empire declined, other momentous events were taking place on the shores of the Aegean. The ancient Greeks traditionally took the fall of Troy, as recounted by Homer, as the starting point of their history. Much academic debate surrounds the exact date of the Trojan War, if indeed it ever took place. Modern archaeologists studying the ruins of Troy have discovered nine superimposed cities, ranging from

HISTORICAL LANDMARKS

c. 660 B.C. Byzantium founded by Byzas the Greek.

A.D. 196 City razed to ground by Septimius Severus.

330 Constantine makes Byzantium the new capital of his empire.

395 Death of Theodosius I; final division of Roman Empire.

413–447 Theodosius II builds new city walls.

527–565 Reign of Justinian the Great.

532–537 Construction of Haghia Sophia.

726–843 Iconoclastic Crisis divides the empire.

11th cent. Seljuk Turks invade Asia Minor.

1204–61 Crusaders sack Constantinople, occupy the city for 57 years.

1326 The Osmanli Turks capture Bursa; the Ottoman Empire is born.

1453 Mehmet the Conqueror captures Constantinople and makes it his capital, renamed Istanbul.

1520–66 Reign of Süleyman the Magnificent.

1683 Ottoman Empire reaches its greatest extent.

18th cent. Ottomans lose territory following series of wars with European powers.

1839–76 Period of reform in Ottoman Empire.

1909 Young Turks depose Sultan Abdül Hamid II.

1922 The Sultanate is abolished.

1923 Turkey becomes a republic; Atatürk elected president.

1938 Death of Kemal Atatürk.

1952 Turkey joins NATO.

1973 Bosphorus Bridge completed.

1993 Tansu Çiller becomes first woman prime minister.

1995 Islamic fundamentalist party, Refah, wins vote.

1998 High court outlaws Refah party.

Troy I (3000–2500 B.C.) to Troy IX (350 B.C.–A.D. 400); the city of King Priam, described in the *Iliad* and the *Odyssey*, is thought to be either Troy VI, which was destroyed by an earthquake in 1275 B.C., or its successor Troy VIIa. Some say the Trojan War never took place at all, and that the decline of Troy was due to the mysterious "Sea People" mentioned earlier.

Whatever really happened, the Mycenaean Greeks who were supposed to have conquered King Priam's city soon found their own civilization in decline. A race known as the Dorians came to power in southern Greece, forcing many mainland Greeks to leave their homeland and cross the Aegean to settle on the coast of Anatolia. Their colonization of the coast took place in successive waves of immigration. First came the Aeolians, who settled the region to the north of Smyrna (now İzmir), then the Ionians, who settled the coast south of Smyrna as far as the River Maeander. The Dorians followed, installing themselves south of the Maeander, in the region known as Caria.

Around 1000 B.C. mainland Greece entered a "dark age" of limited achievements, but not so the Ionians, who developed an outstanding civilization. By the eighth century B.C. the 12 main city-states of Ionia, including Ephesus, Priene, and Miletus, had formed what was known as the Pan-Ionic League. Science, philosophy, and the arts flourished, and the Ionians founded further colonies.

Lydians and Persians

Inland from Ionia lived the wealthy and powerful Lydians, with their capital at Sardis. They reached their peak during the reign of Croesus (560–546 B.C.), who owed his fortune to gold panned from the River Pactolus. His lasting legacy was the invention of coinage, which led to the beginnings of our money-based economy. His expansionism brought the bulk of Ionia under Lydian rule, but also resulted in conflict with the advancing Persians in the east, where he was roundly defeated. Driven back to Sardis, he witnessed the sacking of his city by the army of Cyrus the Great, in 546 B.C.

With Lydia defeated, the Greek coastal cities lay open to the Persians, who swiftly incorporated them into their empire. Ionia's revolt around 499 B.C., supported by Athens, was easily subdued. However, Athenian involvement provoked the Persian king Darius to invade the Greek mainland. He was defeated at the famous Battle of Marathon in 490 B.C., and ten years later his son Xerxes lost the Persian fleet at the Battle of Salamis. Xerxes suffered a further humiliating defeat in 479 B.C., when his army was beaten at Plataea on the same day that his fleet lost to the Greeks at Mycale.

As a result of the Persian Wars, the Greek cities of Anatolia were encouraged to join the Delian Confederacy, paying tribute to Athens in return for protection against the Persians. Athens became so attached to this source of easy money that dissent soon grew among the member cities, and Sparta led the confederacy from Athens after the Peloponnesian War (413–404 B.C.). The Persians, sensing weakness in the ranks, launched another offensive, resulting in the Aegean coast cities coming under Persian control in 387 B.C.

Alexander the Great

Meanwhile, King Philip II of Macedon dreamed of driving out the Persians from northern Greece and unifying the entire Greek world. His dreams were fulfilled, and even surpassed, by his son Alexander the Great, in a brief but action-filled lifetime of only 33 years (356–323 B.C.). In 334 B.C., aged only 22, he led his army across the Hellespont (now the Dardanelles), and paused at Troy to make a sacrifice at the temple of Athena and pay homage to his hero Achilles, before going on to defeat the Persians at the Battle of Granicus and liberating the Ionian cities. After conquering the entire Aegean and Mediterranean coasts of Anatolia, and subduing Syria and Egypt, he took the great prize of Persepolis, the Persian capital, before advancing farther still into India. During his 12-year campaign Alexander established some 70 cities, and built the greatest empire the world had yet seen.

After Alexander the Great's death, the conquered territory was divided among his generals, whose mutual antagonism and expansionist ambitions led to weaknesses that exposed western Anatolia to the increasing might of Rome.

Enter the Romans

One of the most prosperous city-states of the Aegean coast was Pergamum, ruled since 264 B.C. by the Attalid dynasty. The last of the Attalid kings, Attalus III, is remembered as something of an eccentric—one of his hobbies was devising new poisons and testing their efficacy on his reluctant slaves. When he died (of natural causes) in 133 B.C., his subjects were dismayed to learn that he had bequeathed his entire kingdom to the Romans. Thus Pergamum became the capital of the new Roman province of Asia. Mithridates VI, King of Pontus (on the Black Sea), resisted Roman occupation, temporarily occupied Pergamum, and ordered the massacre of all Romans. But eventually Rome's power prevailed in this territory.

In 27 B.C. Julius Caesar's nephew Octavian took the name Augustus; Rome ceased to be a republic, and became an empire. There followed a long period of peace and prosperity known as the Pax Romana. All of Asia Minor (the Roman name for Anatolia) was incorporated into the Roman Empire. Greek cities were embellished with Roman buildings.

Soon, news of a new religion that was beginning to cause trouble for the Roman authorities spread through the empire.

Christianity threatened the establishment because it rejected the old gods and denied the divinity of the emperor. Paul the Apostle carried the word. His voyages (A.D. 40–56) led to the founding of many churches, notably the Seven Churches of Asia addressed in the Revelation of St. John — Pergamum, Smyrna, Ephesus, Thyatira, Laodicea, Sardis, and Philadelphia.

The great fortress of Rumeli Hisari guards the upper reaches of the Bosphorus.

Byzantium

Legend claims that the city of Byzantium was founded around 660 B.C. by a Greek named Byzas, after the Delphic Oracle had bidden him to build his city "opposite the Land of the Blind." When he saw that earlier settlers had built a town on the eastern shore of the Bosphorus, he decided they must have been blind themselves to overlook the advantages of an easily defensible point across the water, and founded Byzantium there, on the site now occupied by Topkapı Palace.

In the succeeding centuries Byzantium, like the cities of the Aegean, fell under the sway of Athens, Sparta, Persia, Alexander, and Rome. It tried to regain its independence from Rome, but proved too small and weak, and was conquered by Emperor Septimius Severus in A.D. 196. He had the city razed to the ground, but soon saw the advantages of its strategic location, and began a programme of enlarging and strengthening the old defensive walls.

A succession of weak and decadent emperors saw the Roman Empire fall gradually into decline and anarchy. In A.D. 286 Diocletian sought to reverse the decline by splitting the administration of the empire in two—he would govern the east, based in Nicodemia, while his friend Maximian ruled the west from Milan—and later to split it further into four parts. His policy succeeded for a time, but following his abdication in A.D. 305, the empire continued to weaken, harassed by invaders and troubled by internal strife. Constantine the Great (who was a convert to Christianity) and Licinius ruled east and west respectively, until in 324 Constantine overthrew his pagan ally and reunited the empire. He chose Byzantium as his new capital to emphasize the break with heathen Rome. The city was inaugurated with great ceremony in 330 and, in honour of the emperor, was renamed Constantinople. Constantine added new city walls, following a plan he claimed to have been given by Christ in a vision, and commissioned a grand central forum decorated with a triumphal column as well as several other monuments. The "New Rome" soon achieved a preeminence in the Christian world that it would retain for 1,000 years.

In 392 the Emperor Theodosius proclaimed Christianity to be the official religion of the Roman Empire, and on his death in 395 the empire was split once more, between his two sons, and was never again to be reunited. The Western Empire, ruled from Rome, fell to the Ostrogoths in 476, while its neighbour, the Eastern, or Byzantine Empire, became one of the longest-lived empires the world has ever known, dating from 395 to 1453.

The greatest of the Byzantine emperors was Justinian the Great (ruler from 527 to 565), who introduced an equitable legal system, and also extended the boundaries of the empire into Spain, Italy, and Africa. He greatly encouraged the arts, and commissioned the building of the magnificent basilica, the Haghia Sophia.

Following the death of the Prophet Mohammed in 632, Arab armies, united under Islam, poured out of their homeland, and soon took Egypt, Syria, and Palestine from the Byzantines; Constantinople was besieged from 674 to 678, but survived because of its defences. The empire was further diminished by the loss of North Africa and Italy, and was brought to the brink of civil war by the Iconoclastic Crisis, before enjoying another brief golden age under Basil II (976–1025). But the empire's troubles increased as invaders made further incursions into Byzantine territory. Most worrying were the Seljuk Turks, who came out of the east in the 11th century to wrest large parts of Asia Minor from Constantinople's control. Converted to Islam in the tenth century, and fired by religious zeal, the Seljuks overran Anatolia, menacing Christian holy places and attacking the pilgrims bound for Jerusalem.

Reluctantly, the Emperor Alexius I sought outside help from the Christian West. The First Crusade was organized to help the Byzantines recapture the Holy Land from the "infidel" Muslims, and resulted in victory for the Crusaders. The Second and Third Crusades, however, were a disaster for the Christians. The Fourth Crusade, launched in 1202 and partly inspired by Venetian jealousy of Byzantium's trading power, became an excuse to plunder Constantinople itself. Thus, the city that had held out against so many attacks by the infidel, became subjected to mindless pillaging by fellow Christians.

The Crusaders ruled the city from 1204 to 1261, calling their new state Romania, also known as the Latin Empire. A remnant of the Byzantine Empire survived in Nicaea (now İznik), and recaptured Constantinople in 1261, but the city had been shattered and its great monuments were stripped of gold, silver, and precious works of art. The place was never the same again.

The Ottomans

During the 14th century the Turks in Anatolia rallied under the banner of one Osman Gazi, who had won a great victory over the Byzantines in 1301. Osman Gazi's son, Orhan, captured Bursa in 1326, and set up his capital there, then moved it to Adrianople (Edirne), which he took in 1361. By the 15th century, the whole of Anatolia and Thrace, except for Constantinople, was under the control of these Osmanli (or Ottoman) Turks. The Byzantine Emperor at the time, Manuel II (1391–1425), tried to appease his enemies by allowing a Turkish district, mosque, and tribunal within his city, and by courting Turkish goodwill with gifts of gold, but to no avail. The young Ottoman Sultan, Mehmet II, who reigned from 1451 to 1481, set about cutting off Constantinople's supply lines. The huge fortress of Rumeli Hisarı on the Bosphorus was built in just four months in 1452. He then withdrew to his capital in Adrianople to await the spring.

The Byzantines tried to protect the Golden Horn from enemy ships by stretching a huge chain across its mouth. They repaired and strengthened the city walls that had saved them so many times in the past, and waited fearfully for the inevitable onslaught. In April 1453 the Sultan's armies massed outside the city walls, outnumbering the Byzantines ten to one. The siege and bombardment lasted seven weeks. The Ottoman admiral bypassed the defensive chain by having his ships dragged overland under cover of darkness, opening a second attack. The final assault came on 29 May 1453, when the Ottoman army surged through a breach in the walls. The last emperor, Constantine XI, fell in the fighting, and by noon that day Mehmet and his men had taken control of the sought-after city.

His first act was to ride to Haghia Sophia and order that it be converted into a mosque; on the following Friday, he attended the first Muslim prayers in what came to be called Ayasofya Camii (Mosque of Haghia Sophia). After allowing his soldiers three days of pillaging, he restored order, acting with considerable leniency and good sense. Henceforth he became known as *"Fatih"* (Conqueror), and his newly won capital city was renamed Istanbul.

Fatih Sultan Mehmet laid claim to all the territories previously held by the Byzantines, so that his empire incorporated most of Greece and the Balkans, as well as Anatolia. Expansion

Mehmet the Conqueror captured Constantinople from the Byzantines in 1453.

continued under his successors, but it was during the reign of his great grandson, Süleyman, that the Ottoman Empire reached its greatest and most celebrated heights. Süleyman the Magnificent, aged 25, ascended the throne and ruled for 46 years (1520–1566), the longest and most glorious reign in the history of the Ottomans. Süleyman's army captured Belgrade in 1521. Rhodes capitulated in 1523. Six years later he besieged Vienna for 24 days (unsuccessfully) before going on to take most of Hungary. Turkish corsairs, notably the infamous Barbarossa, helped to conquer Algiers and Tunis.

By the mid-17th century the Ottoman Empire had reached its greatest extent, stretching from Batumi at the eastern end of the Black Sea to Algeria, taking in

Mesopotamia, Palestine, the shores of the Red Sea (including Mecca and Medina), Egypt, Anatolia, Greece, the Balkans, Hungary, Moldavia, the North African coast, the Crimea, and southern Ukraine. With such far-flung territories, dissolution was inevitable, and began immediately. Northern conquests, including Hungary, had been lost by the close of the 17th century. The decline of these territories was drawn out and painful, leaving problems in its wake that have been the source of trouble and friction in the Balkans and the Middle East ever since.

Decline and Fall

The year 1821 marked the beginning of the Greek War of Independence, which resulted in victory for the Greeks in 1832, and another loss of territory for the Ottomans, whose empire

Completed in 1973, the Bosphorous Bridge was the first bridge ever to link Europe and Asia.

had shrunk significantly. A century of decadence and intermittent wars had left the Ottoman sultanate in serious, irreversible decline. Attempts at reform came too late; by 1876 the government was bankrupt. Sultan Abdül Hamid II (1876–1909) tried to apply absolute rule to an empire staggering under a crushing foreign debt, with a fragmented population of hostile people, and succeeded only in creating ill will and dissatisfaction amongst the younger generation of educated Turks.

Young army officers and the professional classes were becoming increasingly interested in Western ways of government and social organization. European literature was widely studied. Robert College, an American school, and the Galatasaray Lycée, the French Academy in the city, were turning out young men imbued with dreams of democracy. These intellectuals formed an underground group known as the "Young Turks," centred on Salonica, where revolt broke out. In 1909 Abdül Hamid was deposed and replaced by his brother, Mehmet V.

Harem Scarem

When Abdul Hamid was deposed in 1909, the harem was closed down, but no one knew what to do with the women. Finally, their families were notified and all 213 members of the harem were assembled at Topkapı for one of the most bizarre identification parades ever. Rough peasants and silken-clad girls clung together as fathers claimed daughters, and brothers recognized long-lost sisters. Some women could no longer speak their native languages, and others were disappointed as no one came forward to claim them.

In 1970 the last survivor of the harem was still living in a small house in the Princes' Islands. On the rare occasion when she did leave the house she was heavily veiled. No one ever saw her face nor knew her name; she was known only as *Sarayli Hanim*, "the Lady of the Palace."

23

There followed the Balkan Wars, in which Turkey lost western Thrace and Macedonia, then World War I, into which Turkey entered on Germany's side. In the notorious Gallipoli campaign of 1915, the Turks, under the leadership of General Mustafa Kemal, defeated the Allied attack on the Dardanelles.

At the end of the war, the Treaty of Sèvres formally ended the existence of the Ottoman Empire. Greece was given large concessions, Armenia was to become an independent state in the east, and the Middle East was to be divided among the Arab leaders who had fought with Colonel Lawrence (under British and French "spheres of influence").

The subsequent period of internal strife between the Turks and the Greeks and Armenians was dominated by Mustafa Kemal, who had risen from the status of war hero to become the leader of the Turkish nationalist movement. In 1920, with army support, he was elected president of the Grand National Assembly in Ankara in defiance of the Sultan's government in Constantinople. From 1919 to 1922 he waged war with the Greeks, who had invaded at Smyrna, and ultimately managed to defeat them and force their withdrawal from Asia Minor.

He was then faced with the delicate task of abolishing the sultanate without antagonizing the religious elements within his party. This meant deposing Sultan Mehmet VI, who as *caliph* (leader of the Islamic world) and sultan stood for the old tradition of combined secular and religious power. Kemal handled the problem with his usual vigour and eloquence in a speech to the Assembly, by linking the power of the caliphate with that of the Assembly: "… It was by force that the sons of Osman seized the sovereignty and Sultanate of the Turkish nation… Now the Turkish nation has rebelled and has put a stop to these usurpers, and has effectively taken sovereignty and the Sultanate into its own hands. This is an accomplished fact."

Monuments to Atatürk are a common sight throughout Turkey.

In the early morning of 10 November 1922, Mehmet VI slipped quietly away to a waiting British warship, to end his life in exile. He was replaced as *caliph* by his cousin, whose powers were strictly limited by secular laws, until that position, too, was abolished in 1924.

The Republic of Turkey

In 1923 the Treaty of Lausanne defined the present borders of the Turkish Republic. An exchange between Greece and Turkey of expatriate populations resulted in the movement of thousands of people, and the wholesale desertion of Greek villages and districts.

From 1925 to 1935 several wide-ranging reforms were introduced by President Kemal. He secularized institutions, reformed the calendar, adapted the Latin alphabet for the Turkish language, emancipated women, and improved agriculture and industry. He introduced the Western idea of surnames (until then Turks had a single name) and made everyone choose a family name, which they had to hand down to their children. For himself he chose Atatürk, or Father of the Turks.

His proved an appropriate choice, as he almost single-handedly created the modern Turkish state. He was enormously popular with the common Turkish people, and when he died in 1938 thousands of mourners lined the railway track to salute the white presidential train as it carried him from Istanbul for burial in Ankara, the new capital.

Turkey remained neutral during World War II until 1945, when it entered the war on the side of the Allies. It joined NATO in 1952. The Democratic Party was elected in 1950, and remained in control until 1960, when, faced with increasing social and economic difficulties, it was overthrown by a military coup. A new constitution consolidating liberal reforms was drawn up, and approved by a referendum held in 1961. However, further unrest led to more coups in 1971 and 1980, after which yet another, more restrictive, constitution was prepared.

Turgut Özal, leader of the Motherland Party and former world banker and economist, was elected as prime minister in 1983, and served until his death in 1993. Under his leadership Turkey adopted a Western-style economy and in 1987 applied for membership of the European Community (now Union).

He was succeeded by Tansu Çiller, Turkey's first woman leader. She inherited the country's rampant inflation and the conflict between Kurdish separatists and the security forces in the southeast. These political and economic difficulties helped the fundamentalist Refah party later win the largest share of the vote in 1995. The Refah party was officially outlawed in 1998, though it continues to be widely supported. Despite these political tensions, Turkey is becoming an increasingly popular tourist destination, offering all the trappings of a Mediterranean paradise and a wealth of fascinating history.

WHERE TO GO

Modern Istanbul, a sprawling metropolis of more than 10 million inhabitants, is split in two by the narrow, sinuous strait known as the Bosphorus. The historic heart of the city lies on a small peninsula at the south end of the strait, known as Saray Burnu, or Seraglio Point. This easily defensible thumb of land is bounded on three sides by the so-called "Three Seas"—the Sea of Marmara to the south, the Bosphorus to the east, and the Golden Horn to the north. The Old City, also known as Stamboul or Eski Istanbul, spreads across seven hills and is home to the city's richest historic treasures—Haghia Sophia, the Covered Bazaar, the Blue Mosque, Topkapı Palace, the Süleymaniye Mosque, and the Church of St. Saviour in Chora.

The Blue Mosque, surrounded by its signature minarets, rises above the Hippodrome.

The new Galata Bridge spans the mouth of the Golden Horn, linking Old Istanbul to the "New City" of Beyoğlu. Here you will find the 14th-century Galata Tower, the stylish shops, trendy cafés, and luxurious hotels of İstiklal Caddesi and Taksim Square, and the sumptuous splendour of the Dolmabahçe Palace.

Ferries cross the Bosphorus to Üsküdar, and ply the length of the scenic strait, past such pretty fishing villages as Arnavutköy, Kanlıca, Tarabya, and Emirgan, and offering good views of the great fortress of Rumeli Hisarı. To the south, in the Sea of Marmara, lie the woods and beaches of the Princes' Islands.

THE OLD CITY — STAMBOUL

Istanbul's most popular tourist attractions are concentrated in the Sultanahmet district, near the tip of the Saray Burnu peninsula, and are all within easy walking distance of each other. A new tram line runs from Sirkeci, near the Galata Bridge, through Sultanahmet, past the Covered Bazaar, the hotels of Laleli and Aksaray, and on to the city walls at Topkapı bus station (not to be confused with the famous palace of the same name). The outlying sights of St. Saviour in Chora and Yedikule are best reached by taxi.

Sultanahmet District

The Sultanahmet district occupies the summit of the first of the Old City's seven hills. This was the site of the original Byzantium, founded in the seventh century B.C., and of the civic centre of Constantinople, capital of the Byzantine Empire. Here, too, the conquering Ottoman sultans chose to build their most magnificent palaces and mosques. Of the few remains of the Byzantine city, the most remarkable building is the Haghia Sophia.

Haghia Sophia (Ayasofya)

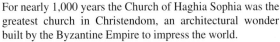

For nearly 1,000 years the Church of Haghia Sophia was the greatest church in Christendom, an architectural wonder built by the Byzantine Empire to impress the world.

It is thought that a Christian basilica was built here in A.D. 325 by the Emperor Constantine, on the site of a pagan temple. It was destroyed by fire in A.D. 404 and rebuilt by Theodosius II, then burnt down again in 532. The building you see today was commissioned by Justinian and completed in 537, although many repairs, additions, and alterations have been made over the centuries. The dome was damaged by earthquakes several times, and the supporting buttresses have coarsened the church's outward appearance.

The finest materials were used in its construction—white marble from the islands of the Marmara, *verd antique* from Thessaly, African yellow marble, gold and silver from Ephesus, and ancient red porphyry columns that possibly came from Egypt and may once have stood in the Temple of the Sun at Baalbek. The interior was covered with golden mosaics, lit by countless flickering candelabras.

The last Christian service ever to be held in Haghia Sophia took place on 28 May 1453, the day before Constantinople finally fell to the

A golden throne: one of the royal treasures of Topkapı Palace.

Turks. Mehmet the Conqueror immediately converted the building to an imperial mosque, and built a brick minaret at the southeast corner. The architect, Sinan, strengthened the buttresses and added the other three minarets during the 16th century; the structure was last renovated in the 1840s. Haghia Sophia served as a mosque until 1935, when Atatürk proclaimed that it should become a museum.

The entrance path leads past the ticket desk to a shady tea-garden outside the main portal, which is surrounded by architectural fragments from the fifth-century church built by Theodosius; an excavated area to the left of the door reveals a part of this earlier building. You enter the Haghia Sophia church through the central portal, across a worn and well polished threshold of *verd antique*, and under a ninth-century mosaic of Christ Pantocrator, into the long, narrow narthex, running to right and left. Note the beautiful matching panels of marble, and the vaulted gold mosaic ceiling. As you continue through the huge bronze doors of the Imperial Gate, your eyes will be drawn skywards by the upwards sweep of the dome. It is about 31 metres (100 feet) in diameter, and stands 55 metres (180 feet) high—the same as a 15-storey building.

The sensation of space is created by the absence of supporting walls beneath the dome; it rests instead upon four great arches, which in turn spring from four massive piers. The arches that flank the nave are filled with tiers of columns and the walls with windows, while the arches above the entrance and the apse are backed by semi-domes, further increasing the interior space. It was the great achievement of the Byzantine architects Isidorus and Anthemius, to transfer the weight of the dome to the pillars using arches and "pendentives," the four triangular sections of masonry that fill the gaps between arches and dome, to create the illusion of an unsupported dome floating in space. The Emperor Justinian

Istanbul Highlights

Haghia Sophia. The highest achievement of Byzantine architecture, and the greatest church in Christendom for nearly 1,000 years. Open 9:30am–5pm, closed Monday (galleries 9:30–11:30am and 1:30–4:30pm). (see page 29)

Topkapı Palace. Attractions include the richly decorated apartments of the Harem, the priceless diamonds and emeralds of the Treasury, and the sacred relics in the Pavilion of the Holy Mantle. Open 9:30am–5pm, closed Tuesday in winter. Harem open 10am–4pm. (see page 33)

Archaeological Museum. One of the best museums in Turkey, famous for its collection of exquisitely preserved sarcophagi. Open 9:30am–5pm, closed Monday. (see page 39)

Grand Bazaar. The world's largest covered market, with over 4,000 shops. Open 8:30am–7pm, closed Sunday. Free. (see page 43)

The Süleymaniye. The finest imperial mosque in Istanbul, a fitting memorial to Süleyman the Magnificent, and to his architect Sinan, the Ottoman Empire's greatest master-builder. Open sunrise to sunset. Donation. (see page 45)

St. Saviour in Chora (Kariye Camii). The beautiful mosaics and frescoes in this former church stand as a monument to the final flowering of Byzantine art in Constantinople. Open 9:30am–5pm, closed Tuesday. (see page 48)

Dolmabahçe Palace. This vast 19th-century palace on the shores of the Bosphorus is a monument to extravagance and excess. Open 9am–4pm, closed Monday and Thursday. Guided tour; charge made for guided tour and video. (see page 58)

The Bosphorus. Ferry tours depart three times a day from Eminönü (check ticket office for departure times). (see page 59)

Büyükada. The largest and most popular of the Princes' Isles is the place to escape from the heat and bustle of the city. Horse-drawn carriages take you on a tour of the pine-clad island. Ferries depart from Eminönü several times daily. (see page 63) was so overwhelmed by the first sight of what his architects had achieved that he cried out, "Glory be to God that I have been judged worthy of such a work! O Solomon, I have surpassed you!"

The original decoration has long since disappeared. Eight huge medallions, bearing the Arabic names of Allah, Mohammed, two of his grandsons, and the first four caliphs, and a quotation from the Koran in the crown of the dome, are remnants of Haghia Sophia's 500 years of service as an imperial mosque, as are the elaborate *mihrab* and *mimber* in the apse. But a few Christian **mosaics** survive—above the apse is the Virgin with the infant Jesus, with the Archangel Gabriel to the right (his companion Michael, to the left, has vanished save for a few feathers from his wings).

The best mosaics are in the galleries, reached by a spiral ramp at the north end of the narthex. By the south wall is the famous **Deesis,** an extraordinary 13th-century mosaic show-

Topkapı Palace features a series of courtyards linked by ceremonial gates.

ing Christ flanked by the Virgin Mary and St. John the Baptist. On the east wall are two images showing Byzantine emperors and emperesses making offerings to Christ on his throne (to the left), and to the Virgin and Child.

At the east end of the galleries, two small columns and a circle of green marble mark the spot where the empress sat during services; on the floor of the nave below, a circle of coloured stone to the right of centre is the **Opus Alexandrinum,** the place where the Byzantine emperors were crowned. Retrace your steps down the ramp and through the first door on your left. In front of you is the **Weeping Column,** or the Column of St. Gregory, which has a thumb-sized hole covered with a brass plate. If you insert a finger, it comes out damp—the moisture is known to have miraculous healing powers, especially for eye diseases.

As you leave by the door at the south end of the narthex, turn round and look up above the door to see a beautiful tenth-century **mosaic** of an emperor and empress offering symbols of Haghia Sophia and Constantinople to the Virgin Mary and Child.

Topkapı Palace (Topkapı Sarayı)

Between Haghia Sophia and the tip of Saray Burnu stretches the walled enclosure of Topkapı Palace, the former residence and seat of government of the Ottoman sultans. Begun in 1462 by Mehmet the Conqueror, it was enlarged and extended by each succeeding sultan until it became a miniature city, which included mosques, libraries, stables, kitchens, schools, the imperial mint, treasuries, barracks, armouries, government offices, and audience halls. At its height it supported a population of nearly 4,000.

Sultan Abdül Mecit moved into the newly built Dolmabahçe Palace in 1853 (see page 58), and by 1909 Topkapı was completely abandoned. In 1924 it was converted to a museum, and has been undergoing a continuous programme of restoration ever since. It is the city's most popular tourist attraction, and deserves a full day to do it justice. If pushed for time, the "must-sees" are, in order of importance, the Harem, the Treasury, and the Pavilion of the Holy Mantle.

The palace is laid out as a series of courtyards linked by ceremonial gates. You enter through the **Imperial Gate** (built in 1478) into the wooded gardens of the First Court. On the left is the Byzantine church of **Haghia Eirene** (Divine Peace), rebuilt together with Haghia Sophia after being burnt down in 532 (closed to the public). This area was also known as the **Court of the Janissaries,** after the crack military corps that served as the sultan's bodyguard and used it as an assembly ground while on duty at the palace (the name derives from the Turkish *yeni çeri*, meaning "new army"). It originally contained the palace bakery, the armoury, and the mint. At the far right-hand corner is the ticket office, which originally served as a prison. The fountain is called the Executioner's Fountain, because here he rinsed his sword and washed his hands after carrying out his orders; examples of his handiwork were displayed on pikes at the Imperial Gate.

Buy your ticket and pass through the turreted Gate of Salutations, better known as the Orta Kapı, or **Middle Gate.** Only the sultan was permitted to ride through this gate on horseback; all others had to dismount and bow. It leads into the Second Court, also known as the **Court of the Divan,** because the Imperial Council (known as the Divan) governed the Ottoman Empire from here. Five avenues radiate from the inside of the gate. To the right lie the enormous **Palace Kitchens,** which house a collection of European crystal, Chinese porcelain, Ottoman serving dishes, and cooking imple-

Interior of the Topkapı Harem, once home to the Sultan, his mother, his wives, and his concubines.

ments. Straight ahead is the ornate Gate of the White Eunuchs, which leads into the Third Court, and the private quarters of the palace. The avenue on the left leads towards the pointed **Divan Tower** (*Divan Kulesi*), at the foot of which lie the Council Chamber and the Grand Vezir's Office. Here, too, is the entrance to Topkapı's main attraction, the Harem.

The **Harem** housed the private quarters of the sultan, his mother, and his many wives and concubines. Its dim network of staircases, corridors, and courtyards linked the sumptuously decorated chambers of the royal household, and harboured a claustrophobic world of ambition, jealousy, and intrigue. The Harem, open from 10:00 A.M. to 4:00 P.M., can be visited only on the official 30-minute guided tour (offered in English and other languages), for which you must buy an additional ticket. Try to get there early, as tours sell out quickly on busy days. The ticket will be stamped with the time your tour begins,

A painting of the Sultan and his court on display in Topkapı Palace.

which may be immediately, or a few hours later—ask when you buy. The tours are rushed, and the route may vary due to restoration work.

You enter by the **Carriage Gate,** where, on the rare occasions they were permitted outside, the women mounted their carriages. The only adult males allowed in the Harem were the Black Eunuchs, who were in charge of security and administration. Their quarters opened off the narrow **Courtyard of the Black Eunuchs,** beyond the gate. Windows in the colonnade on the left give a glimpse of their tiny rooms; sticks hanging on the walls were used to beat miscreants on the soles of their feet, a mandatory punishment for all novices.

A long, narrow corridor lined with shelves (for trays of food) leads to the Courtyard of the Women Servants, from which you enter the **Apartments of the Valide Sultan** (the sultan's mother, who was the most powerful woman in the Harem). Her domed Sitting Room is panelled with 17th-century Kütahya tiles, and decorated with scenic views. A raised platform framed by two columns contains divans and a low dining table. The door on the left, beyond the hearth, leads to the valide sultan's bedchamber, with a gilded bed canopy and ornate floral faïence in turquoise, blue, and red. A small adjoining prayer room has scenes of Mecca and Medina.

The right-hand door leads to the **Apartments of the Sultan** himself. First you pass the entrance to the royal bath chambers, designed by Sinan and richly ornamented in marble. There are paired but separate chambers for the sultan and the valide sultan, each having a changing room, a cool room, and a hot room. The sultan was bathed by elderly female servants, then dried and pampered by groups of younger handmaidens.

The Harem Hierarchy

The bottom rung of the Harem ladder was occupied by the *cariye*, a concubine of the lowest rank. Taken from their families as girls of 12 years old, either captured in war, kidnapped, or even bought as slaves, they came from the non-Muslim parts of the empire (religion forbade the enslavement of a Muslim woman). Many were from Circassia (in the western Caucasus mountains), whose women were noted for their black hair and fair skin. The girls were taught Turkish and Arabic, music, dancing, and etiquette, and converted to Islam.

If a *cariye* caught the sultan's eye, she became a *gözde* (favourite), was given servants and a private room, and set about winning an invitation to the sultan's bedchamber. If she succeeded she received the title *ikbal* (success), and if she bore a child, she was a *haseki* (that which belongs to the sultan).

Next move (an option only if she bore a male child) was to become a *kadın*, one of the four "official" wives permitted by the laws of Islam. A *Kadin* was given a whole suite of rooms and a retinue of slaves. As a *kadın* the young woman's aim was to become *valide sultan* (mother of the new sultan), the undisputed queen of the Harem, and often the power behind the throne.

Next, you enter the vast and splendid **Imperial Hall,** with three handsome marble fountains, and a canopied throne from which the sultan would enjoy the music and dancing of his concubines. The valide sultan and the senior wives sat on sofas under the gallery to the left, while the more talented slave-girls played music from the balcony above.

Perhaps the most splendid of all the rooms is the **Salon of Murat III,** with inlaid floors, flowered İznik tiles of the best period, carved fountains, canopied sofas, and a superb domed ceiling, designed by Sinan. On the far side a door leads to the Library of Ahmet I, with cupboard doors and shutters inlaid with mother-of-pearl and tortoiseshell, which in turn opens into the dining room of Ahmet III, better known simply as the **Fruit Room.** This tiny, wood-panelled room is covered all over with lacquered paintings of flowers and fruit in rococo style. Ahmet III was known as the "Tulip King," and celebrated each spring with a tulip festival in the palace grounds.

The exit from the Harem opens into the **Third Court,** otherwise reached through the Gate of the White Eunuchs. Immediately inside the gate is the richly decorated **Throne Room** (*Arz Odası*), where the sultan received foreign ambassadors. Head down to the right to the **Treasury,** whose chief attractions are the famous golden Topkapı Dagger, with three huge emeralds set in the hilt, and a fourth forming the lid of a watch hidden in the handle; and The Spoonmaker's Diamond, an 86-carat, pear-shaped diamond set in a gold mount encrusted with 49 smaller diamonds. Other exhibits include gilded thrones studded with precious stones, a pair of solid gold candlesticks set with 666 diamonds (one for each verse of the Koran), and reliquaries containing the hand and part of the skull of John the Baptist.

Across the courtyard is the magnificently decorated **Pavilion of the Holy Mantle,** which houses sacred relics of the Prophet Mohammed, and is therefore a place of great religious importance for Muslims. The **Fourth Court** contains a number of pretty pavilions and terraces, and a restaurant and cafeteria with fine views of the Bosphorus.

Topkapı Museums

From Topkapı's First Court, a narrow cobbled lane leads to the Fifth Court, which contains three excellent museums. The **Archaeological Museum** (Arkeoloji Müzesi) has been expanded to include galleries devoted to Cyprus, Syria and Palestine, the Phrygians, Troy, and Anatolia, from the Palaeolithic to the Iron Age. Its main attraction, however, is the magnificent collection of sarcophagi, especially the Alexander Sarcophagus, decorated with scenes of hunting and battle.

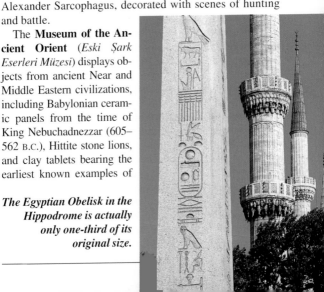

The **Museum of the Ancient Orient** (*Eski Şark Eserleri Müzesi*) displays objects from ancient Near and Middle Eastern civilizations, including Babylonian ceramic panels from the time of King Nebuchadnezzar (605–562 B.C.), Hittite stone lions, and clay tablets bearing the earliest known examples of

The Egyptian Obelisk in the Hippodrome is actually only one-third of its original size.

writing (2700 B.C.), and the oldest recorded set of laws, the
Code of Hammurabi (1750 B.C.).

Built in 1472 for Mehmet the Conqueror, and decorated
with turquoise and blue tile, the most eye-catching building in the square is the **Tiled Kiosk** (*Çinili Köskü*). It
houses a valuable display of ceramics ranging from Seljuk
times to the present.

Hippodrome

The long, narrow park stretching southwest from Haghia
Sophia is known as the **Hippodrome** (At Meydanı), and in
Byzantine times that's exactly what it was. Inspired by the
Circus Maximus in Rome, it was built in A.D. 203 as a stadi-
um for chariot-racing and other public events. Later it was
enlarged by Constantine the Great, eventually measuring
400 metres long by 120 metres wide (1,300 feet by 400 feet),
and could hold an audience of 100,000.

The Hippodrome was the setting for the ceremony which
proclaimed Constantinople as the "New Rome" in A.D. 330,
following the division of the Roman Empire, and soon became
the civic centre of the Byzantine capital, decorated with imposing monuments and flanked by fine buildings. Unfortunately it
was destroyed when the city was sacked during the Fourth
Crusade, and left stripped of its statues and marble seats. In the
17th century its ruins were used as a quarry for the building of
the Blue Mosque (see page 41). Only its outline, a few brick
vaults, and three fine ancient monuments survive today.

The north end of the *spina*, or central axis, is now marked by
an ornate domed ablutions fountain, given to the city by Germany's Kaiser Wilhelm II to commemorate his visit in 1900.
At the opposite end rise the three remnants of the original Hippodrome. The **Egyptian Obelisk,** brought to Constantinople
by the Emperor Theodosius in A.D. 390, had been commis-

sioned by the pharaoh Thutmose III in the 16th century B.C. What you see is only the top third of the original—it broke during shipment. The reliefs on the pedestal show Theodosius and his family in the Hippodrome (on the side opposite the Serpentine Column) presiding over the raising of the obelisk.

The **Serpentine Column** consists of three intertwined bronze snakes; they originally supported a gold vase, but the snakes' heads and the vase have long since disappeared. It is the oldest Greek monument in Istanbul, commemorating the Greek victory over the Persians at Plataea in 479 B.C. (it was brought here from Delphi by Constantine the Great). A second, deeply eroded stone obelisk is known as the **Column of Constantine Porphyrogenitus,** as an inscription on its base records that the emperor of that name (A.D. 913–959) had it restored and sheathed in gilded bronze plates.

The six minarets of the **Blue Mosque** dominate the skyline of the Hippodrome. Known in Turkish as the *Sultan Ahmet Camii* (Mosque of Sultan Ahmet), it was built between 1609 and 1616 for the Sultan Ahmet I, after which it became the city's principal imperial mosque because of its proximity to the sultan's palace at Topkapı. To savour the full effect of the architect's skill, enter the courtyard through the gate which opens onto the Hippodrome. As you pass through the portal, the façade sweeps up in front of you in a fine crescendo of domes. (Go out through the door on the left of the courtyard to reach the entrance for tourists which leads to the mosque proper.)

Once inside, you will see how the mosque earned its familiar name. The very air seems to be blue—more than 20,000 turquoise İznik tiles glow gently in the light from the mosque's 260 windows, decorated with lilies, carnations, tulips, and roses. Four massive columns support a dome 22 metres (70 feet) in diameter, and 43 metres (142 feet) high at

the crown—big, but not quite as big as Haghia Sophia, the de-
sign of which obviously influenced the architect. The *mihrab*
and *mimber* are of delicately carved white marble, and the
ebony window shutters are inlaid with ivory and mother-of-
pearl. The painted blue arabesques in the domes and upper
walls are restorations; to see the original version, look at the
wall beneath the sultan's loge.

Across from the Hippodrome and the Blue Mosque is the
Museum of Turkish and Islamic Arts (*Türk ve İslam Eserleri Müzesi*). The collection, housed in the former palace of
Ibrahim Paşa, the son-in-law of Süleyman the Magnificent,
includes illuminated Korans, inlaid Koran boxes, antique
carpets, ceramics, and Persian miniatures. The ethnographic
section has tableaux of a nomad tent, a yurt, a village house,
and a traditional carpet loom, with explanations of the natural dyes used to colour the wool.

Across the tram lines from Haghia Sophia lies the entrance to one of Istanbul's more unusual historic sights—the
Yerebatan Sarayı (Underground Palace). This amazing
construction is actually an underground cistern, one of many
that once stored Constantinople's water supply. Aqueducts
brought the water from the Belgrade Forest, north of the city,
to the cisterns, where it was held in reserve in the event the
city was besieged. The cistern measures 140 metres (460
feet) by 70 metres (230 feet); its vaulted brick roof is supported by a forest of columns topped by Corinthian capitals,
336 in all, set in 12 rows of 28. As you peer into the dripping
gloom, you can marvel at the fact that it still stands, 1,500
years after it was built.

Central District

The street with the tram lines that lead uphill from Sultanahmet (Divan Yolu) was, and still is, the main road leading to

the city gates in Byzantine and Ottoman times. The next tram stop is called Çemberlitaş (Hooped Column), after the stone pillar that rises to the right of the road. Also called the **Burnt Column,** it was charred and cracked by a great fire that ravaged the district in 1770 (the iron hoops help to reinforce the column). Constantine erected it in A.D. 330 to mark the city's new status as capital of the Eastern Roman Empire. Parts of the Cross and the nails with which Christ was crucified are reputed to be sealed in the column's base.

The Grand Bazaar

Behind the Burnt Column rises the Baroque exterior of the Nuruosmaniye Camii (built in 1755). Walk towards it, then turn left through an arched gate into the mosque precinct, and follow the crowds into the bustling **Grand Bazaar.** The Kapalı Çarşı (Covered Market) of Istanbul is the world's largest covered bazaar, with about 4,000 shops, as well as banks, cafés, restaurants, mosques, and a post office, crammed together in a grid of 66 narrow streets that total 8 km (5 miles) in length —all protected from summer sun and winter rain by a multitude of domed and vaulted roofs. Mehmet the Conqueror built the first covered market on this site in 1461. It has been rebuilt several times after destruction by fire and

A coffee peddler fills a customer's cup at the Grand Bazaar.

The Beyazıt Tower was originally built as a fire lookout point.

earthquake, most recently in 1954, and again, to a lesser degree, in 1974.

It is fairly easy to find your way, as most of the streets follow a pattern and are well signposted. From the Nuruosmaniye entrance, stretching towards the **Beyazıt Gate,** is the main street, lined with jewellers' shops. On your right is the entrance to the 16th-century **Sandal Bedesten,** with lovely brick vaults supported on massive stone pillars. It is quiet and empty for most of the week, but comes alive during the auctions held here at 1:00 P.M. on Tuesdays, Wednesdays, and Thursdays. In the centre of the bazaar is the **Old Bedesten,** where you can find the best quality gold and silver jewellery, brass and copper ware, curios, and antiques (the most precious goods were traditionally kept in the Bedesten, as it can be locked securely).

The Beyazıt Gate, at the far end of the main street (*Kalpakçılar Başı Caddesi*), leads to a street of vegetable and flower stalls. Turn right, and first left up the stairs to the **Book Market** (*Sahaflar Çarşısı*), a shady retreat and popular place for university folk. There is a selection of English books, including many titles devoted to Turkish history, art, and architecture.

Beyazıt

Beyond the Book Market lies **Beyazıt Meydanı,** a vast, pigeon-thronged square below the entrance to Istanbul University. Over the weekend the square hosts a flea market, where vendors lay out a variety of new and second-hand goods. Old men sell bags of corn for you to feed to the pigeons, while brightly dressed water-sellers tout for business with cries of *"buz gibi!"* ("ice-cold!"), and encourage tourists to take a photograph—for a fee, of course.

The east side of the square is dominated by the beautiful **Beyazıt Camii,** built in the early 16th century by Sultan Beyazıt II, son of Mehmet the Conqueror. It is the earliest surviving example of classical Ottoman architecture, inspired by Haghia Sophia (see page 29). Opposite the mosque is the arched gateway to Istanbul University and the 50-metre (148-foot) **Beyazıt Tower,** built in 1828 as a fire-lookout point.

The Süleymaniye

The outline of the Süleymaniye, the **Mosque of Süleyman the Magnificent,** rises from a site above the Golden Horn (near the north gate of Istanbul University). Deemed the finest Ottoman building in Istanbul, the mosque is a tribute to the "Golden Age" of the Ottoman Empire, and to the two great men of genius who created it—Sultan Süleyman I, the Magnificent, and his chief architect, Sinan. Süleyman, known in Turkish as Kanuni (The Lawgiver), reigned from 1520 to 1566, during which period the empire attained the height of its wealth and power.

The Süleymaniye and its extensive complex of attendant buildings was built between 1550 and 1557, a task that employed around 5,300 labourers and craftsmen. Legend has it that jewels from Persia were ground up and mixed in with the mortar for one of the minarets, and that the incredible acoustics were achieved by embedding 64 hollow clay vessels facing neck-down in the dome. It is also said that Süleyman, in awe of his architect's achievement, handed the keys to Sinan at the inauguration ceremony and allowed him the privilege of opening it.

You enter through a courtyard, colonnaded with grand columns of granite, marble, and porphyry, with a rectangular şadırvan (ablutions fountain) in the centre. The interior is vast and inspiring, flooded with light from the 16th-century stained-glass windows. The mosque is square in plan, about 58 metres (172 feet) on a side, capped by a dome 27½ metres (82 feet) in diameter and 47 metres (140 feet) high. The tiles are original İznik faïence, with floral designs; the woodwork of the doors and shutters is delicately inlaid with ivory and mother-of-pearl.

Both Süleyman and Sinan (the latter lived to be almost 100) are buried nearby. The tombs of the sultan and his wife Roxelana lie behind the mosque in the walled garden, an atmospheric spot, where roses and hollyhocks tangle among the tall grass between the gravestones, and flocks of sparrows swoop and squabble in the fig trees. Sinan's modest tomb, which he designed himself, stands in a triangular garden at the northern corner of the complex, capped by a small dome.

A walk around the terrace beside the mosque, which affords a fine view across the Golden Horn, will give you some idea of the huge size of the complex. You can also look up at the four magnificent minarets said to signify that Süleyman was the fourth sultan to reign in Istanbul, and the ten balconies remind us that he was the tenth ruler of the Ottoman dynasty.

Outer Stamboul

There are a number of worthwhile sights between the Süleymaniye and the city walls, but they are scattered and you will want to use taxis to reach most of them. Away from the main roads, these mostly residential districts contain a maze of back streets, muddy lanes, and cobbled alleys. The odd old wooden house that has survived the city's numerous fires leans creaking across the crumbling bricks of some forgotten Byzantine ruin. If you choose to walk, be prepared to get lost, often, and to be an object of friendly curiosity.

The imposing **Şehzade Camii** (Mosque of the Prince), which overlooks a grassy park that is unfortunately spoilt by traffic noise, one of Sinan's early works (1548), was built in memory of Süleyman the Magnificent's son, Prince Mehmet, who died in 1543 aged 21.

Spanning the park and the six lanes of the busy thorough-fare Atatürk Bulvarı are the ruins of the **Aqueduct of Valens** (*Bozdoğan Kemeri*), originating back in the second century A.D. It was rebuilt by the Emperor Valens in the fourth century, restored several times by both the Byzantines and Ottomans, and remained in use up to as recently as the 19th century.

If you follow the line of the aqueduct away from the city centre, you will soon reach the vast complex of the **Fatih Camii** (Mosque of the Conqueror), perched on top of the city's Fourth Hill. It was the first imperial mosque to be built following the Conquest of Constantinople in 1453, and its *külliye* (mosque complex), the biggest in the whole of the Ottoman Empire, included a hospital, poorhouses, a mental asylum, visitors' accommodation, and a number of schools teaching science, mathematics, history, and Koranic studies. At the time, such enlightened education was unusual anywhere in the world. Built by Mehmet the Conqueror between 1462 and 1470, the complex was almost completely destroyed by an earthquake in 1766. Only the courtyard and its huge portal survived; the rest was rebuilt. The tombs of the Conqueror and his wife are in the walled graveyard behind the mosque.

Farther out, dominating the Fifth Hill, is the **Sultan Selim Camii** (Mosque of Selim I), dedicated to the father of Süleyman the Magnificent. Unlike its dedicatee, who was known as *Yavuz Selim* (Selim the Grim), the mosque is one of the most charming in the city, with a sparse but tasteful decoration of beautiful İznik tiles from the earliest period in turquoise, blue, and yellow, and richly painted woodwork. Its dramatic situation overlooking the Golden Horn commands a fine, sweeping view across the picturesque districts of Fener and Balat.

The brightest jewel in Istanbul's Byzantine crown is the former church of **St. Saviour in Chora,** known in Turkish as the **Kariye Camii.** Restored and opened as a museum in 1958, this small building, tucked away in a quiet corner of the city, is one of the world's greatest monuments to Byzantine art. The church's name means "in the country," because the first one to be built on this site was outside the city walls. Although it was later enclosed within the Theodosian Walls, the name stuck.

St. Savior in Chora appears as a reflection in the window of a sidewalk café.

The oldest part of the existing building, the central domed area, dates from 1120. The church was rebuilt and decorated early in the 14th century under the supervision of Theodore Metochites, an art-lover, statesman, and scholar who was a close friend and advisor of the Emperor Andronicus II Palaeologus. Sadly, Metochites was reduced to poverty and sent into exile when the emperor was overthrown in 1328. He was allowed to return to the city in 1330 provided that he remained a monk at Chora, which he did, living out the last years of his life surrounded by the magnificent works of art he had commissioned.

Metochites left the central portion of the church intact, but he added the outer narthex and the parecclesion (side chapel). The wonderful mosaics and frescoes, dating from between 1310 and 1320 (contemporary with those of Giotto in Italy), are almost certainly the work of a single artist, now unknown. Their subtlety of colour, liveliness of posture, and strong, lifelike faces record a last remarkable flowering of Byzantine art before its descent into decadence. The church was converted into a mosque in 1511, but fortunately it was not substantially altered. The mosaics were covered with wooden screens, some windows were boarded up, and a minaret was added.

The **mosaics** are grouped into four narrative cycles depicting the lives of Christ and the Virgin Mary, along with portraits of various saints, and large dedicatory panels. The mosaic above the door leading from the narthex into the nave shows the figure of Metochites, wearing a huge hat, offering a model of his beloved church to Christ. Each tiny tile is set at a different angle to its neighbours so that the reflected light creates the illusion of a shimmering, ethereal image.

The **frescoes** are all in the parecclesion, which stretches the length of the building and was used in Byzantine times as a funerary chapel. The artist's masterpiece is the *Anastasis* (Resurrection) in the vault of the apse, showing Christ pulling Adam and Eve from their tombs, while the figure of Satan lies bound and helpless beneath His feet.

Fifteen minutes' walk from the Kariye, and marking the summit of the Sixth Hill, is the **Mihrimah Sultan Camii,** built by Sinan in 1565 for Süleyman's favourite daughter. Next to the mosque are the **Theodosian Walls,** pierced here by the **Adrianople Gate** (*Edirnekapı*), where Mehmet the Conqueror entered the fallen city in 1453. The double walls, built in the fifth century, during the reign of the Emperor Theodosius, stretch 6½ km (4 miles) from the Sea of Marmara to the Golden Horn. They were defended by 96 towers and had numerous gates. Much of the inner wall and several of the towers are still standing. Seven gates are still in use.

At the Marmara end of the Theodosian Walls, a long way from the city's other sights but easily reached by bus or taxi, stands the ancient fortress of **Yedikule** (Seven Towers). It encloses the famous **Golden Gate** (*Altınkapı*), the grand triumphal arch of the Byzantine emperors, which existed before the walls were built and was incorporated into them. In 1470 Mehmet the Conqueror further strengthened the ancient portal by building three towers of his own, linked by curtain walls to the four Byzantine towers flanking the Golden Gate. During Ottoman times the fortress was used as a prison and a treasury.

The Golden Horn (Haliç)

The Golden Horn is an inlet of the Bosphorus, penetrating 7½ km (4½ miles) into the hills behind the city. It forms a natural harbour, and in Ottoman times was the site of the Imperial Tershane (Naval Arsenal), capable of holding 120 ships. Today it is lined with shipyards, factories, and industrial development, and its waters are badly polluted.

Eminönü

The mouth of the Golden Horn is spanned by the busy **Galata Bridge.** The first bridge here was a wooden structure, built in 1845. It was replaced in 1910 by the famous old pontoon bridge with its seafood restaurants, which served until the present bridge was opened in 1992. Like the Atatürk Bridge farther upstream, its central span opens daily at 4:00 A.M. to allow ships in and out.

At the Stamboul end of the bridge is the colourful district of Eminönü, a major transport hub where bus, ferry, tram, and train services interconnect. At rush hour, the waterfront becomes a bedlam of bodies as commuters pour off the ferries. The air is loud with blasts from ships' horns, and the water boils white as half a dozen vessels jostle for a vacant berth. Smaller boats equipped with cooking fires and frying pans bounce around in the wash, while their crews dish up mackerel sandwiches to hungry workers standing on the quayside, seemingly oblivious to the violent, churning movement of their floating kitchens. Adding to the activity are the sellers of grilled corn cobs, *lahmacun*, *simit*, and fried mussels, who compete with the kitchen boats for pass-

---

The Spice of Life

At the Spice Bazaar in Eminönü, sellers once sat cross-legged on carpets, ready to seize pestle and mortar for pounding potions both efficacious and fanciful, optimistically prepared to cure anything from lumbago to love sickness through to highly complicated cases of combatting the Evil Eye. Nor were they all charlatans—some of the market's herbal remedies are still available, even though they no longer contain such rare (or interesting) ingredients as ambergris, dragon's blood, or tortoise eggs.

---

ing trade while the water-sellers tempt thirsty diners with lemon- and cherry-flavoured drinks.

The wide square opposite the bridge is dominated by the **Yeni Camii** (New Mosque). Commissioned in 1597 by the Valide Sultan Safiye, mother of Mehmet III, it was not completed until 1663, making the Yeni Camii the youngest of Istanbul's classical mosques.

The large archway to the right of the mosque is the entrance to the famous **Spice Bazaar,** also known as the **Egyptian Bazaar** (*Mısır Çarşısı*). It was opened a few years before the Yeni Camii, and its revenues originally paid for repairs to the mosque complex. Inside, the air is heady with the mingled aromas of ginger, pepper, cinnamon, cloves, and freshly ground coffee. The L-shaped building has 88 shops, many still devoted to the sale of spices, herbs and herbal remedies, but dried fruit and nuts, *lokum* (Turkish Delight), fresh fruit and flowers, apple tea, and more mundane household items

occupy most stalls.

If you leave the Spice Bazaar by the gate at the far end of the first aisle and then turn right, you will find the **Rüstempaşa Camii** (Mosque of Rüstem Paşa), with its minaret soaring high above the narrow back street. This is one of Sinan's smaller works, and one of his most beautiful. The interior is al-

The myriad scents of the Spice Bazaar mount an olfactory assault on visitors.

most completely covered in İznik tiles of the finest period, with floral and geometric designs in blue, turquoise, and coral red.

Eyüp

Ferries depart from the upstream side of the Galata Bridge for the half-hour trip along the Golden Horn to the suburb of **Eyüp,** which contains one of Islam's most sacred shrines. The **Eyüp Sultan Camii** (mosque) marks the burial place of Eyüp Ensari, the standard-bearer of the Prophet Mohammed. He died in battle while carrying the banner of Islam during the Arab siege of Constantinople, between A.D. 674 and 678. Following the conquest in 1453, his grave was rediscovered, and Mehmet the Conqueror erected a shrine on the spot, followed in 1458 by a mosque, the first to be built in Istanbul. Thereafter each sultan, on his accession, visited Eyüp Camii to gird himself ceremonially with the Sword of Osman, the first Ottoman sultan. The original mosque was destroyed by an earthquake in 1766; the present building dates from 1800.

The Tomb of Eyüp Ensari, opposite the mosque, is decorated with gold, silver, and coloured tiles, and is protected by a gilded grille. Remember that this is a sacred place—dress respectfully (long trousers or long skirt and long-sleeved shirt; women should cover their heads, shoulders, and arms), remove your shoes before entering, and do not use your camera.

Behind the mosque, on the hill, is a vast cemetery littered with turbanned headstones. A path winds up to the **Pierre Loti Café,** named in honour of the 19th-century French writer who once lived in the neighbourhood, and who wrote a number of romantic novels about life in Istanbul. The café enjoys a splendid view down the Golden Horn to the distant and distinct domes and minarets of Stamboul.

THE NEW CITY—BEYOGLU

The north shore of the Golden Horn was traditionally the quarter where craftsmen, foreign merchants, and diplomats made their homes, beginning in the 11th century when the Genoese founded a trading colony in the district of Galata. Following the Conquest, European ambassadors built their mansions on the hills beyond Galata, a place which came to be called Pera (Greek for "beyond"). Foreigners from the entire Ottoman Empire flooded into Galata and Pera, attracted by the wealth and sophistication of the capital. As the area became increasingly crowded, the wealthy foreign merchants and diplomats moved farther out along the "Grande Rue de Pera" (now İstiklal Caddesi), forming a focus for the 19th- and 20th-century expansion of the modern, European-style part of Istanbul, known as Beyoğlu.

Galata and Pera

As you cross the Galata Bridge, crowded with shoppers, office workers, water-sellers, and anglers, your eyes are drawn naturally to the pointed turret of the Galata Tower. Sometime during the 11th century a rough bunch of coastal traders and drifters from every port in the Mediterranean began to settle on the northern shore of the Horn, in the maritime quarter which became known as Galata.

The **Galata Tower** (*Galata Kulesi*) was the keystone in the colony's defences. Its age is uncertain, but it seems to have been built in its present form around 1349, at the highest point of the city walls. Now restored, with a restaurant and nightclub at the top, it offers a superb panoramic view over the city (open daily 10:00 A.M.–6:00 P.M.). If you look across the Golden Horn, you can count the minarets and domes which embellish Istanbul's famous skyline. From left to right they are: Haghia Sophia; the Blue Mosque; the Nuruosmaniye (above the Galata Bridge); Beyazıt Camii; the Beyazıt Tower; the Süleymaniye, looming over the far shore; the Şehzade Camii (in the distance); the Aqueduct of Valens; the twin minarets of the Fatih Camii (above the Atatürk Bridge); and the Sultan Selim Camii.

To avoid the steep climb up the hill beyond the Galata Bridge take the **Tünel,** the world's oldest (and probably shortest) underground railway, built in 1875. The trip to the top station takes just 90 seconds

The Galata Tower, originally built for defence, now houses a restaurant and nightclub.

(see page 126). To reach the Galata Tower from the top station, turn left out of the exit and immediately left down a very steep road. Follow your nose for about five minutes until you see a sign saying *"Kuledibi"* on the left, which points the way to the tower.

From the Tünel exit, restored 1920s street-cars clang their way along **İstiklal Caddesi** (street), once lined with the palatial embassies of foreign powers. The mansions have been downgraded to consulates since the capital was transferred to Ankara in 1923, and modern shops and restaurants have sprung up. The street is now a pedestrian precinct, and boasts some of the city's most stylish cafés. At

Galatasaray Square, where İstiklal Caddesi bends to the right, an elegant wrought-iron gateway marks the entrance to the 19th-century **Galatasaray Lisesi,** the Franco-Turkish *lycée* (secondary school) that educated many of the great names in modern Turkish history. (The district also shares its name with one of Turkey's famous football clubs.)

Past the square on the left is the entrance to **Çiçek Pasajı** (Flower Alley), a high, glass-roofed arcade lined with bars and restaurants. It is liveliest in the evenings, when the tables fill with a mixture of Turks and tourists. The opposite end of the passage leads into the **Balık Pazarı** (Fish Market), a block of narrow streets lined with stalls selling fish, fruit and vegetables, and a local speciality snack—fried mussels on a stick (*midye tava*).

Turn left at Galatasaray Square, and left again at the British Consulate along Meşrutiyet Caddesi, and you will reach the **Pera Palas Hotel,** established in 1892 to provide accommodation for Orient Express passengers. Its splendour is a little faded now, but that only adds to the charm of

The End of a Dynasty

It is appropriate that Dolmabahçe Palace, the main financial drain that contributed to the downfall of the Empire in 1875, was witness to the final act of the Empire.

When Atatürk's government abolished the Sultanate in November 1922, Mehmet VI, the last representative of the dynasty that had ruled the Ottoman Empire for six centuries, was ignominiously smuggled aboard a British warship anchored off Dolmabahçe, to spend his last years in exile. Atatürk died in the Palace on 10 November 1938 at 9:05 A.M., the hour all the palace clocks were stopped.

the huge, chandeliered, sumptuous public rooms decorated with antique mirrors, braziers, samovars, and thick Turkish carpets. The old bird-cage lift will take you up to the second-floor museum for a look at the suite used by Atatürk.

Taksim

Beyond Çiçek Pasajı, the side streets off İstiklal Caddesi are the focus for Istanbul's raunchier nightlife, packed with seedy bars, "adult" cinemas, and nightclubs—best avoided, unless you want to spend all your money at once. The street ends at **Taksim Square** (Taksim Meydanı), the heart of modern Istanbul, lined with luxurious five-star hotels and the glass-fronted **Atatürk Cultural Centre** (Atatürk Kültür Sarayè), also called the Opera House. It is the main venue for the International Istanbul Festival (see page 89).

At the far end of the square, Cumhuriyet Caddesi leads past the Hilton Hotel to the **Military Museum** (*Askeri Müze*). The fascinating exhibits include a section of the massive chain that the Byzantines used to stretch across the mouth of the Golden Horn to keep out enemy ships, as well as captured enemy cannon and military banners, the campaign tents from which the Ottoman sultans controlled their armies, and examples of uniforms, armour, and weapons from the earliest days of the Empire down to the 20th century. The main attraction is the concert given by the **Janissary Band** (*Mehter Takımı*) at 3:00 P.M. Wednesday through Sunday. The band is a revival of the Ottoman military band that accompanied the sultans' armies on their campaigns and led the victory processions through the conquered cities. The colourful uniforms are exact replicas of the originals, as is the distinctive Janissary march, with the musicians turning to left and right at each alternate step.

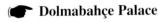 **Dolmabahçe Palace**

Sultan Abdül Mecit (reigned 1839–1861), continuing the programme of reform begun by his father Mahmut II, decided that Topkapı Palace was too old-fashioned for a Westernizing ruler such as himself. He therefore commissioned a vast new palace on the shores of the Bosphorus, on the site of a park that had been created by filling in an old harbour —(dolmabahçe means "filled-in garden"). The **Dolmabahçe Palace** (Dolmabahçe Sarayı; Dolmabahçe Cadessi, tel. 212/258-5544), finished in 1853, was intended as a bold statement of the sultan's faith in the future of his empire, but instead it turned out to be a monument to folly and extravagance. Its construction nearly emptied the imperial treasury, and the running costs came to £2 million a year, a burden that led to the Empire's bankruptcy in 1875.

The guided tour of the palace is in two parts—first the *Selamlık* (public rooms) and Throne Room, then the *Harem* (private apartments). The interior of the palace is very dark, and the use of flash is forbidden, so photographers should think twice before paying the extra fee for bringing in a camera or video equipment.

The highlights of the *Selamlık* include the vast Baccarat and Bohemian crystal chandeliers, 36 in all, and the crystal balustrade of the main staircase, the sultan's marble and alabaster bathroom, two huge bearskins (a gift from the Tsar of Russia), Sèvres vases, Gobelin tapestries and carpets, and the vast bed used by the "giant sultan," Abdül Aziz. The Throne Room is huge—the ceiling is 40 metres (130 feet) high—and lavishly decorated. The chandelier, a gift from Queen Victoria, has 750 light bulbs.

Just 2 km (1.2 miles) beyond Dolmabahçe you can escape from the city among the wooded walks of **Yıldız**

Park. Head up the hill to the **Malta Köskü,** a restored royal pavilion that has been converted into a café, and enjoy tea and pastries on a beautiful terrace looking over the treetops to the Bosphorus.

Nearby is the **Şale Köskü** (Chalet Pavilion), set among beautiful gardens. It was built by Abdül Hamid II in 1882 for the sultan's guests on state visits, but Abdül Hamid liked it so much that he lived there himself until he was deposed in 1909. Its main claim to fame is that it contains the world's largest hand-made carpet (guided tours only, 9:30 A.M.–5:00 P.M., closed Monday and Thursday).

ALONG THE BOSPHORUS

The Bosphorus (Istanbul Boğazı) is the narrow strait linking the Black Sea to the Sea of Marmara, and separating the European part of Turkey from the vast hinterland of Anatolia. The winding channel is 30 km (18 miles) long and about 2 km (1½ miles) wide, narrowing to 750 metres (2,250 feet) at Rumeli Hisarı.

The name Bosphorus is derived from the mythological character Io, who swam across the strait after being turned into a heifer by Zeus (Bosphorus means "ford of the ox" in Greek). Jason and the Argonauts traveled through the strait in their search for the Golden Fleece, and the Persian army of King Darius crossed on a bridge of boats in 512 B.C. en route to battle with the Scythians.

Today the strait is busy with commercial shipping, ferries, and fishing boats, and its wooded shores are lined with pretty fishing villages, old Ottoman mansions, and the villas of Istanbul's wealthier citizens. It is spanned by two impressive suspension bridges. The first bridge ever to link Europe and Asia was the **Bosphorus Bridge** (*Boğağziçi Köprüsü*) at Ortaköy, opened in 1973, and at that time the fourth longest in the world (1,074 metres/3,524 feet). It was followed in 1988 by the **Fatih Sultan Mehmet Bridge** at Rumeli Hisarı.

Special **ferry tours** of the Bosphorus depart three times a day from the jetty at Eminönü (see page 125), calling at villages like Beşiktaş, Kanlıca, Yeniköy, Sarıyer, and Anadolu Kavağı. You can remain on the boat for the round trip, or disembark anywhere and return by bus or taxi.

☛ The Bosphorus Tour

The ship leaves the crowded quay at Eminönü and heads north, past the dazzling white wedding-cake façades of the **Dolmabahçe Palace** and the neighbouring Çirağan Palace, gutted by fire in 1910 but now restored as a luxury hotel. After stopping at **Beşiktaş,** you pass beneath the first of the huge suspension bridges connecting Europe and Asia.

A panoramic view of the city can be savoured from the top of Galata Tower.

Tucked beneath the western end of the Bosphorus Bridge is the village of **Ortaköy,** recognizable by its distinctively Baroque mosque right on the waterfront. The village has a rather Bohemian atmosphere, with shops, art galleries, bookstalls, and cafés. Beyond the bridge, on the opposite shore, is the **Beylerbeyi Palace,** a summer residence and hunting lodge built for Sultan Abdül Aziz in 1865 (guided tours 9:30 A.M.–4:00 P.M., closed Monday and Thursday).

If you head north past the rich suburbs of Arnavutköy and Bebek, you will soon reach the massive fortress of **Rumeli Hisarı** (9:30 A.M. to 5:00 P.M., closed Monday). It was built at the command of Mehmet II in 1452 in preparation for his last assault on Constantinople, and was completed in only four months. Its walls enclose a pleasant park with an open-air theatre that stages folk-dancing and concerts in summer.

On the opposite shore is the smaller and older fortress of **Anadolu Hisarı,** dating from 1390. South of the fort is the ornate rococo façade of the **Küçüksu Lodge,** an Ottoman summerhouse built on a favourite picnic spot known as the Sweet Waters of Asia.

Beyond the Fatih Sultan Mehmet Bridge the boat stops at **Kanlıca** on the Asian shore, famous for its yoghurt, which you can sample at one of the little waterside cafés. The upper reaches of the Bosphorus are lined with picturesque fishing villages—**Tarabya, Sarıyer,** and **Rumeli Kavağı**—where you can enjoy a meal at one of the many excellent seafood restaurants.

You can also visit the **Sadberk Hanım Museum,** with its private collection covering the period from 500 B.C. to Ottoman times. Last stop is **Anadolu Kavağı** on the Asian side, overlooked by a castle built by the Byzantines.

Üsküdar

Directly opposite Stamboul lies Üsküdar, better known as Scutari to Europeans. The ferry from Eminönü passes the **Kız Kulesi** (Maiden's Tower), perched on a tiny island about 200 metres (600 feet) offshore. Originally a 12th-century Byzantine fort, the present tower dates from the 18th century, and has served as a lighthouse, customs office, and control tower. In Byzantine times a huge chain could be slung between here and Saray Burnu to close the mouth of the Bosphorus.

The ferry leaves you at Üsküdar's main square, İskele Meydanı. Note the **İskele Camii,** designed by Sinan in 1548 for Mihrimah, daughter of Süleyman the Magnificent, and the **Yeni Valide Camii** from the early 18th century. West of the square is Sinan's **Şemşi Paşa Camii** (1580).

Scutari is traditionally associated with the name of Florence Nightingale. During the Crimean War (1854–56) she set up a hospital in the huge **Selimiye Barracks** (*Selimiye Kışlası*). A small corner of the building is kept as a museum in her memory—the exhibits include the lamp that gave her her nickname.

Just inland from the Bosphorus Bridge is park and lookout point **Büyük Çamlıca,** capped by a distinctive TV transmitter.

☞ THE PRINCES' ISLANDS

An hour's ferry-trip to the southwest of Istanbul lies the bucolic retreat of the Princes' Islands, known to the Turks simply as Adalar, "The Islands." This archipelago of nine islands in the Sea of Marmara has been inhabited ever since Byzantine times by monastic communities, and was used as a place of exile for deposed rulers. The Emperor Justin II built a palace on the largest island in the sixth century; it soon came to be known as Prinkipo, the Prince's Isle, and the name later spread to cover the whole group.

The Princes' Islands, often a soothing respite from the hustle and bustle of Istanbul.

Today the islands' pretty beaches provide the perfect weekend retreat location for the people of Istanbul. Cars are banned, and all transport is by foot, bicycle, or horse-drawn carriage.

The biggest and most popular island is **Büyükada** (Big Island), with a pleasant town and a picturesque monastery. You can take a tour of the island on a *fayton* (carriage)—to find the "cab rank," walk uphill from the jetty to the clock tower in the square and turn left. The tour will take you past **St. George's Monastery,** where you can sample the monks' home-made wine as well as the healing waters of an *ayazma* (sacred spring). The iron rings in the marble floor of the chapel were used to restrain the mentally ill, who were once brought here hoping to be cured by the waters. The ferry also calls at the smaller islands of **Kınalıada, Burgazada,** and **Heybeliada.**

EXCURSIONS

Bursa

Rich turquoise tiles from İznik adorn the walls of the Green Tomb in Bursa.

The historic city of Bursa lies scattered across the wooded slopes of Uludağ, meaning Great Mountain, to the south of the Sea of Marmara. It was founded in the third century B.C. by King Prusias of Bithynia, and named Prusa in his honour. In 1326 it was taken by Orhan Gazi, and became the first capital of the new Ottoman Empire. Although the capital was moved to Edirne in 1362, and then to Istanbul, Bursa remained an important town, with a rich legacy of religious architecture—the founder of the Ottoman dynasty and five of his successors are buried here. Other attractions include hot springs, a market, and the forests and ski-slopes of nearby Uludağ.

Bursa's most famous building is the **Yeşil Türbe** (Green Tomb), which takes its name from the beautiful tiles that cover its walls. It houses the sarcophagus of Mehmet I (ruled 1413–21), itself ornately decorated with patterned İznik tiles. Below the tomb is the **Yeşil Camii** (Green Mosque), commissioned by Mehmet I in 1419. It is unfinished, as work on a mosque traditionally stopped after the death of the sultan who began it. Despite this the interior is still breathtakingly beautiful, decorated with the best tiles.

The town's **Museum of Turkish and Islamic Art** (*Türk ve İslam Eserleri Müzesi*) is just next to the mosque. This museum displays Karagöz shadow puppets, made from coloured, translucent camelskin. Although this type of shadow play probably originated in China, the stories which made it popular in Turkey were based on the exploits of two Bursa peasants. Karagöz and Hacivat were fellow labourers whose practical jokes incurred the wrath of Sultan Orhan. They were put to death on his orders, but their earthy humour lives on in the puppet plays that became popular throughout Turkey, and especially in Bursa.

The pedestrian plaza in the city centre is bounded at one end by the **Ulu Camii** (Great Mosque), built in the 14th century with stone quarried from Uludağ. It has a rectangular prayer hall capped by 20 domes, supported by 12 great pillars — compare this to the imperial mosques of Istanbul, which reflect the influence of Haghia Sophia. An archway leads from the centre of the plaza into the **Koza Hanı,** an arcaded *caravanserai* (an inn) built in the 15th century and which today is the centre of Bursa's silk trade. In June you can watch dealers haggling over heaps of white silkworm cocoons.

Beyond the *caravanserai* is the town's **Covered Market,** which is as interesting to explore as Istanbul's.

You can enjoy a fine view over the city from the terrace park that holds the **tombs of Orhan and Osman Gazi.** Osman Gazi was the founder of the House of Osman, the

An elderly priest ruminates in a quiet corner at a mosque in Bursa.

dynasty that ruled the Ottoman Empire for 600 years. He died in 1324 in the neighbouring town of Söğüt, but was buried in Bursa in 1326 after the city had been captured by his son, Orhan Gazi. Osman's tomb was formerly a Byzantine baptistery, and his son's tomb is in the nave of the neighbouring church—fragments of its ancient mosaic pavement can be seen on the floor of the tomb.

More imperial tombs can be seen at the **Muradiye complex,** which comprises a fragrant rose garden with a mosque and several *türbes*, including that of Sultan Murat II (ruled 1421–1451). His earth-filled sarcophagus lies beneath an opening in the crown of the dome, so that his grave can be washed clean when it rains.

AEGEAN COAST

Turkey's Aegean coast is one of Europe's most popular holiday destinations, offering an unparalleled combination of

The beaches of Kuşadasi are as beautiful as the surrounding waters.

natural beauty and historical interest. This was one of the most densely populated parts of the ancient world, with many famous cities to its name — Troy, city of the *Iliad* and the *Odyssey,* and Smyrna, the birthplace of Homer; Sardis, home of the wealthy King Croesus; Ephesus, where St. Paul preached the gospels; and Halicarnassus, birthplace of the historian Herodotus. The ruins of two of the Seven Wonders of the World — the Temple of Artemis at Ephesus, and the Mausoleum of Halicarnassus — are also to be found here.

Set amid this wealth of historic sites are many beautiful beaches and pretty fishing villages, and a number of modern holiday resorts, notably Kuşadası (see page 75) and Bodrum (see page 79). The principal city in the region is İzmir (ancient Smyrna), which has an international airport.

Gallipoli

The Gallipoli Peninsula (Gelibolu Yarımadası), on the north side of the Dardanelles, was the scene of one of the most notorious military campaigns of World War I. The Allied assault, involving Australian, British, New Zealand, and French forces, aimed to capture the peninsula and control the narrow strait of the Dardanelles, thus securing an ice-free sea passage to supply arms to Russia and open a front against the Germans.

The first landings took place on 25 April 1915, and met with fierce resistance from the Turks, under the leadership of General Mustafa Kemal. The Allies only managed to gain a toehold on the peninsula, and then deadlock ensued, with nearly nine months of static trench warfare. The cost in human lives was terrible, with 250,000 dead and wounded on each side. The Anzacs (Australia and New Zealand Army Corps) saw some of the worst fighting and suffered the heaviest casualties; the beach where they landed has been named Anzac Cove (*Anzak Köyü*) in their honour.

The whole peninsula is a memorial, with plaques describing the campaign's progress, and monuments to the soldiers of the Allied and Turkish armies. Each war cemetery is signposted, and all are beautifully tended, planted with flowers and scented with fragrant hedges of rosemary. Travel agents in Çanakkale, across the strait, provide guided tours of the peninsula. A memorial service is held each year on Anzac Day (25 April).

Troy

The exact location of the legendary city of Troy remained a mystery until an amateur archaeologist with a passion for Homer began excavations in 1871. Heinrich Schliemann found his fabled city, and discovered **"Priam's treasure,"** a cache of gold beside the city walls. He smuggled it back to Germany, but it vanished during World War II, only to make a dramatic reappearance in Moscow in 1993.

Archaeologists have now uncovered nine superimposed cities, from Troy I, an Early Bronze Age settlement (3000–2500 B.C.) to the Hellenistic and Roman metropolis, known as Ilium Novum, which stood here from 334 B.C. to A.D. 400. American scholars identify the level known as Troy VIIa as King Priam's city, and place its destruction around 1260 B.C.; certain eminent Turkish archaeologists disagree, instead opting for the preceding level, Troy VI.

The site, near the village of **Hısarlık,** is marked by a large modern replica of the famed wooden horse. The excavations are actually less impressive than those at most other Turkish sites, but for those who have enjoyed Homer's *Iliad* and *Odyssey* it is a magical place, where the stones are haunted by the spirits of Helen and Paris, Achilles, and Agamemnon.

Pergamum

At the height of its power, in the second century B.C., Pergamum was one of the most splendid cities on the Aegean coast. Its acropolis was capped with magnificent buildings, and it boasted a great library of over 200,000 volumes (the Pergamenes are credited with the invention of parchment). Its ruins, perched high above the modern town of Bergama, are still impressive.

The **acropolis** was built on a set of terraces. On the left of the entrance ramp is the open space once occupied by the **Temple of Athena,** close to which are the remains of the **Pergamene library.** Its contents were eventually given to the beautiful Cleopatra as a gift from Mark Antony, and went to enrich the famous library of Alexandria.

Beyond the library is the city's most splendid building, its glittering white marble columns, now partly restored. The **Trajaneum** was erected during the second century A.D. in honour of the deified emperors Trajan and Hadrian.

The Trojan Horse

Most people know the story of the Trojan War as Homer told it. It all started when peace-loving King Priam's son, Paris, was inveigled by a trio of jealous goddesses into abducting the most beautiful woman in the world, Helen, wife of Menelaus, king of Sparta.

The ensuing war between Greece and Troy lasted 10 years and cost the lives of great heroes such as Hector and Achilles. The end came when the Greeks tricked the Trojans into accepting a gift of a huge wooden horse within their walls—it was filled with armed men who sacked the city and left it in ruins.

Below the Temple of Athena is the steep *cavea* of the **theatre,** set in a shallow depression in the hillside. Nearby is the base of the **Altar of Zeus,** built to commemorate the defeat of the Gauls by the Romans in 190 B.C. This was once decorated with a remarkable frieze depicting the Battle of the Gods and Giants, one of the finest existing examples of Hellenistic sculpture, which now resides in Berlin's Pergamon Museum.

Visible on the plain below is the **Asclepion,** one of the ancient world's leading medical centres, rivalling similar establishments at Epidauros, Kos, and Ephesus. Dedicated to Asclepius, god of healing, the Asclepion provided hot baths, massages, dream interpretation, primitive psychiatry, and draughts of water from a sacred spring (found to be mildly radioactive). Galen (A.D. 130–200), the most famous physician in the ancient world after Hippocrates, practised here.

The entrance to the Asclepion is located along a colonnaded street, the Sacred Way, which leads to the **medical precinct.** Here you can see the remains of the library, theatre, and treatment rooms. In the middle of the square is a pool fed by the sacred spring.

The Bergama **Archaeological Museum,** with a large collection of material from Stone Age to Byzantine times, is in the centre of the modern town.

Sardis

The site of Sardis, the former capital of ancient Lydia, is situated 100 km (60 miles) east of İzmir, on the road to Uşak and Afyon. The Lydians invented coinage, producing the first-ever coins of gold and silver, stamped with the royal emblem: a lion's head. The gold was washed down from the hills by the River Pactolus; the Greek historian Herodotus relates how flakes of the precious metal were trapped in the fleece of sheepskins spread in the stream-bed, perhaps giving rise to the legend of the Golden Fleece.

Sardis was once the wealthiest city in the world, under the famous King Croesus (reigned 560–546 B.C.), hence the expression "rich as Croesus." Intent on expanding his empire into Persian-held territory, he consulted the oracle at Delphi. It told him that if he attacked the Persians he would destroy a great empire. He attacked anyway, and was crushed—the empire he destroyed was his own. The monuments you see today date from Roman and Byzantine times.

The principal ruins of Sardis are in two parts. On the left side of the main highway you will find the **Gymnasium complex.** From the car park you follow a line of **ancient shops** to a gate at the far end, which leads into the **synagogue,** whose floor is richly decorated with mosaic patterns. The gymnasium itself, a huge open square, is dominated by the magnificently restored **Marble Court,** lined with ornate marble columns and niches which once held statues. The arched gateway leads to a large swimming pool and the ruins of a Roman and Byzantine **baths** complex.

In the nearby village, a side road leads south for 1 km (½ mile) to the imposing **Temple of Artemis,** begun during the reign of Alexander the Great, and abandoned, unfinished, following the ascendancy of Christianity in the fourth century. The enormous structure had a peristyle of 52 columns, of which two still stand at their full height. A small fifth-century Byzantine church hides behind the columns at the far end.

İzmir

Known to the Greeks as Smyrna, and to the Turks as *"Güzel İzmir"* (Beautiful İzmir), Turkey's third-largest city sprawls around the head of the finest natural harbour on the Aegean coast. The city was founded in the third millennium B.C. on the north shore of the bay, and reached a peak during the tenth century B.C., when it was one of the most important cities in the Ionian Federation—the poet Homer was born in Smyrna during this period. After the Lydian conquest of the sixth century B.C. the city lost its importance, but was re-founded by Alexander the Great on the slopes of Mount Pagus (now Kadifekale), and under the Greeks and Romans it became one of the principal centres of Mediterranean trade.

When the Ottoman Turks took control in the 15th century, İzmir grew wealthy as a merchant city, handling Smyrna figs and Turkish tobacco from the farms of the interior, and al-lowing the establishment of European trading colonies. It prospered as a Levantine port until the close of the Greco-Turkish War in 1922, when it was almost completely de-stroyed by fire. Rebuilt around the site of Alexander's city, it

The Saat Kulesi (Clock Tower) marks the Konak Meydanı in the heart of İzmir.

is once again a bustling port and industrial town, but almost
no trace remains of its former glory.

The heart of the city is **Konak Meydanı,** a busy pedestrian
square distinguished by two famous monuments. The **Saat
Kulesi** (Clock Tower), dating from 1901, is the unofficial symbol of İzmir. Nearby stands the tiny **Konak Camii** (mosque),
built in 1756 and decorated with colourful Kütahya tile panels.
On the hill to the south of the square stands the **Archaeological
Museum,** whose superb collection of antiquities includes statues of Poseidon and Demeter that once stood in the Agora of
ancient Smyrna. The Ethnographic Museum, opposite, recre-
ates the interiors of traditional local houses. Inland from the
Konak Mosque is İzmir's **bazaar,** one of the best in Turkey.

North of Konak Meydanı, **Atatürk Caddesi** (also known
as the **Kordon**) runs along the waterfront to the ferry port at
Alsancak, 3 km (2 miles) away. A horse-drawn phaeton will
take you on a tour, which passes through **Cumhuriyet Meydanı** (Republic Square), the centre of modern İzmir, surrounded by glittering luxury hotels and palm-fringed promenades.
Nearby is the **Kültür Parkı,** a huge, shady pleasure garden,
venue of the annual International Fair. Uphill to the south of
the park lies the **Agora,** one of the few remaining traces of
İzmir's ancient history. This colonnaded square, built during
the second century A.D., was once the city's bustling market-
place. At the top of the hill is the imposing medieval fortress of
Kadifekale. This was the ancient Mount Pagus, where Alexander the Great commanded his generals Lysimachus and
Antigonus to found a new city back in the fourth century B.C.
However, no trace remains of their original fortifications.

Çeşme

A six-lane toll motorway leads 80 km (50 miles) west of İzmir
to the small resort and ferry port of Çeşme, where boats cross

daily to the Greek island of Chios, a mere 12 km (7½ miles) away. The town was a quiet spa and beach resort (its name means "drinking fountain") until the motorway's arrival brought it within comfortable commuting distance of the city; now it is set to become a bustling seaside suburb of İzmir, and a terminal for international ferries from Italy and Greece.

The town is dominated by a Genoese **fortress** built in the 14th century, and enlarged by the Ottomans. Beside the fortress lies an 18th-century **caravanserai,** or inn, which has been converted into a hotel, and now hosts regular "folklore evenings" of Turkish dance and music. On the main shopping street you will find an attractive and interesting art gallery housed in the ancient Greek basilica of Ayios Haralambos.

There are a few other sights to see—the main attractions are the golden-sand **beaches** at Altinkum and Ilıca, and the **hot springs.** The warm, sulphurous waters (around 35–50°C/95–122°F) are said to be good for treating rheumatism and respiratory complaints.

The small resort and ferry port of Çeşme sends boats daily to the nearby Greek island of Chios.

Kuşadası

Situated on a small promontory, Kuşadası, meaning "Island of Birds," is one of Turkey's liveliest and most popular holiday resorts. The town, 80 km (50 miles) south of İzmir, has a large yachting marina, and serves as a port for Mediterranean cruise ships. Attractions here include some pleasant beaches,

The haunting ruins of Ephesus on Kuşadasi.

a vibrant nightlife, and the nearby ruins of Ephesus.

White-washed houses climb the hill above the harbour, where ferries depart daily for the Greek island of Samos, and lively bars and restaurants line the streets of the old quarter. The busy **bazaar** clusters around the walls of a 17th-century *caravanserai*, now converted into a hotel; across the street, seafood restaurants skirt the quay of the old harbour.

Beyond the modern ferry port, a 350-metre (1,050-foot) causeway connects Kuşadası to **Güvercin Adası** (Pigeon Island), which is topped by a 13th-century Byzantine castle and ringed with gardens and colourful cafés.

A dolmuş service links the town to Ladies' Beach (Kadınlar Plajı) 3 km (2 miles) to the south, and there are also beaches at **Pamucak** and in the **Dilek National Park** (Dilek Yarımadası Milli Parkı), 25 km (15½ miles) from town.

Ephesus (Efes)

Ephesus, 17 km (10½ miles) inland from Kuşadası, is one of the best-preserved and most visited of Turkey's ancient cities. Its marble streets and monuments have been extensively exca-

Chess is a popular pastime on Kuşadasi.

vated and restored by archaeologists, and with only a little imagination it is easy to transport yourself to Roman times.

Ionian Greeks from the island of Samos settled in Ephesus around 1000 B.C. The site was associated with the worship of the Anatolian mother-goddess Cybele, who became merged with the Greek Artemis. The great Temple of Artemis, one of the Seven Wonders of the World, was erected in her honour. The city was ruled in turn by the Lydians, the Persians, and the Attalid kings of Pergamum, until 133 B.C., when Attalus III bequeathed his kingdom, and Ephesus with it, to the Romans. Ephesus was one of the most important cities in the new Province of Asia, with a population of 200,000, and grew wealthy on the proceeds of trade. But its greatness was linked to its fine natural harbour, and when this silted up in the third century A.D. the city went into decline. The site was rediscovered by a British archaeologist in 1869 after six years of searching. Many of the ruins that you see today date from the Roman period, between the first century B.C. and second century A.D.

Most of the guided tours commence at the **Magnesian Gate** and head downhill along the main street. The first buildings inside the gate are the well-preserved **Odeum** (council chamber). Its semi-circular seats, and the **Prytaneum,** where archaeologists found two statues of Artemis, now on display in the Selçuk Museum. The marble-paved **Street of the Curetes,** stone rutted by ancient cart wheels, leads through the Gate of Hercules to the remarkable **Temple of Hadrian,** with an arched doorway capped by the head of Tyche, goddess of fortune. At the corner of Marble Street, on the right, are the **Baths of Scholastica,** which also included a brothel.

Rising up ahead is the imposing façade of the **Library of Celsus,** built in A.D. 110 by a Roman consul as a memorial to his father, and restored during the 1970s. Beautiful statues of the four virtues—Episteme (Knowledge), Sophia (Wisdom), Ennoia (Thought), and Arete (Valour)—adorn the niches between the columns.

Marble Street leads from the library to the **Great Theatre,** the probable setting for the riot of the silversmiths described in the Bible (Acts 19:24–41). Its vast *cavea* provided seating for 25,000 people, and still accommodates the crowds who gather for performances during the annual Ephesus International Festival (see page 89). From the top rows of seats you can enjoy a grand view of the Arcadian Way, the city's colonnaded main street, once lined with fine statues, and lit by oil lamps at night. At its far end a scrub-filled depression marks the site of the former harbour, long since silted up.

The small town of **Selçuk,** about 5 km (3 miles) from Ephesus, has an interesting **museum** and several noteworthy monuments. The sixth-century **Basilica of St. John,** on Ayasuluk Hill, marks the site of the Apostle's tomb. The fortress above dates from Byzantine times. Downhill you will find the impressive **Isa Bey Mosque** (1375), and beyond is a solitary column marking the site of the once-great **Temple of Artemis.**

Legend has it that St. John the Apostle brought the Virgin Mary to Ephesus around A.D. 37–48. Situated at **Meryemana** (Mother Mary) in the hills above the city is the house where she is thought to have passed the last years of her life. It was discovered during the 19th century by priests from İzmir following instructions given by a German nun, Anna Katharina Emmerich, who had seen it in a vision. There is now a chapel occupying the site, which has long been a place of pilgrimage, but the building's foundations may date from the first century.

South from Ephesus

Between Selçuk and Bodrum lie three important archaeological sites that can all be easily seen in one day.

Priene, once one of the most active ports in the Ionian Federation, now stands about 5 km (3 miles) inland, due to the silting up of the River Maeander. It enjoys a beautiful location on a terrace overlooking the plain, backed by the steep crag of the acropolis. The theatre, *bouleterion* (council chamber), and agora are worth exploring, but the main attraction is the great **Temple of Athena.** Alexander the Great, who passed through the city in 334 B.C., paid for its completion; five of the original 30 columns have been restored to their full height.

The silt of the River Maeander has also stranded the once-mighty city of **Miletus.** Its harbour, from which Milesian ships set forth to found over 100 colonies during the seventh and eighth centuries B.C., is now a frog-filled marsh. Some inkling of its former glory can be gleaned from the ruins of the agora, the theatre, and the Baths of Faustina.

The most impressive of the three sites is **Didyma.** No city ever stood here, just the colossal **Temple of Apollo,** one of the largest and most elegant temples in the ancient world. Only two columns still stand, but the forest of massive marble stumps gives some idea of the grandeur of the original building. People would travel great distances to consult the oracle of Apollo, seeking advice on business issues, marriage, and military campaigns. When the Persians destroyed Miletus in 494 B.C. they also razed the Temple of Apollo at

Didyma. Its reconstruction was begun by Alexander the Great (his decisive victory over the Persians at Gaugamela in 331 B.C. was predicted by the oracle), and continued for many centuries, but the temple was never completed; note that some of the columns remain unfluted.

Bodrum

The picture-postcard resort of Bodrum occupies the site of ancient Halicarnassus, famed as the city of King Mausolus (whose tomb was one of the Seven Wonders of the World), as well as the birthplace of Herodotus, the "Father of History." Little remains of Halicarnassus, however, and the town's main attractions include its laid-back, bohemian atmosphere, a beautiful double bay backed by whitewashed houses, and the magnificent **Crusader Castle** that dominates the harbour. No wonder it has been dubbed the Saint

The town of Hisarlik, near ancient Troy, is distinguished by a replica of the Trojan Horse.

Floodlights illuminate the Castle of St. Peter
as night falls on Bodrum.

Tropez of Turkey. The attractions of Bodrum, however, have not gone unnoticed—during the summer months it is very crowded and very noisy, and more international in flavour than Turkish.

The **Castle of St. Peter** was built in the 15th century by the Knights of St. John, who used stone that had been quarried from the ruins of the Mausoleum of Halicarnassus. It fell to the Ottomans in 1523, and its various buildings now house a fine collection of antiquities, including a fascinating **Museum of Underwater Archaeology.** The various towers offer splendid views across the town and harbour. In the **English Tower** the banqueting hall has been restored, and you can sip a glass of Turkish wine while you entertain yourself and read the centuries-old graffiti carved in the window niches by homesick knights who stayed here.

The site of the **Mausoleum,** the tomb of King Mausolus, is set a few blocks in from the harbour. It was begun around 355 B.C. at the behest of the king (the word "mausoleum" is derived from his name) and remained standing until at least the 12th century. By the time the Crusaders arrived in 1402 it was in ruins, destroyed by an earthquake. Today, nothing remains except the foundations. An exhibition hall displays several versions as to how the building may have previously looked, and plaster-casts of the friezes that once decorated its walls; the originals are in the British Museum in London.

There are no good beaches in Bodrum itself, which could be an advantage, as you have more choice if you take a **boat trip** from the harbour to one of the many coves that lie hidden along the coast of the peninsula to the west, or catch a *dolmuş* to a selection of pretty fishing villages: namely Turgutreis, Gümüşlük, Yalıkavak, and Türkbükü.

Pamukkale

One of the most popular excursions from the Aegean resorts goes to the spectacular travertine terraces of Pamukkale (the Cotton Castle), which lie above the town of **Denizli,** about 200 km (125 miles) inland from Kuşadası.

This remarkable natural formation has been created by mineral-rich hot springs cascading down the hillside and depositing layers of calcium carbonate. The resulting pools, terraces, and "petrified waterfalls" of dazzling white travertine are one of Turkey's most famous sights.

The ruins of ancient Hierapolis lie scattered on the hillside above the terraces, adding historical interest to natural beauty. In the grounds of the Pamukkale Motel you can bathe in the **Sacred Pool,** where the therapeutic, restorative spring waters will float you above a picturesque jumble of broken columns and Corinthian capitals.

A trip to Pamukkale usually includes a visit to the site of the ancient city of **Aphrodisias.** The city, dedicated to the worship of Aphrodite, goddess of love, was famous for its superb sculpture. The ruins, which are still being excavated, include one of the best-preserved stadia in Turkey, 228 metres (748 feet) long, with seating for 30,000, and the remarkable Sebasteion, a porticoed gallery of sculpture dedicated to Aphrodite and to the Roman Emperor.

Bathers enjoy the mineral waters among the fallen columns of Pamukkale's Sacred Pool.

WHAT TO DO

SHOPPING

Istanbul's markets and bazaars offer some of the world's most interesting—and challenging—opportunities for shopping. A huge variety of hand-made goods finds its way into the city from towns and villages all over Turkey, much of it of very high quality—wool and silk carpets, kilims (flat-weave rugs), cicims (embroidered kilims), leather goods, ceramics and pottery, copper and brassware, and jewellery. There is also, of course, a lot of poorer-quality merchandise aimed specifically at the tourist market, notably in the big coastal resorts.

The principal shopping area in Istanbul is, undoubtedly, the **Grand Bazaar,** with more than 4,000 shops crammed beneath its roof. Running downhill from here is Uzunçarşı Caddesi, lined with hardware shops, which leads to the Spice Bazaar, the best place to buy *lokum* (Turkish Delight). The weekend flea-market in Beyazıt Square is an interesting place to browse, and there are bargains to be found among the bric-a-brac. Across from the square are the back streets of Laleli, the place to look for low-priced clothes. For more modern, upmarket shopping, you can join Istanbul's jet-set in the stylish boutiques of Nişantaşı and Teşvikiye, near Taksim Square, or head west to the Galleria shopping mall by the marina at Ataköy. For craft shops, antiques dealers, and galleries, take a stroll around Ortaköy on a Saturday or Sunday.

Shops are generally open from 9:30 A.M. to 7:00 P.M. Monday to Saturday, and closed over lunch from 1:00 to 2:00 P.M., though many tourist shops stay open later and on Sundays. The Grand Bazaar is open 8:00 A.M. to 7:00 P.M., Monday to Saturday.

Bargaining

In an economy where many products are hand-made, each item has a different value depending on the quality of workmanship it shows. Bargaining is thus a way of determining an appropriate price, not simply a way for the shopkeeper to get more money from the buyer. To get the best price, though, you must get to know the market by browsing in several shops and asking the prices of comparable pieces.

The Grand Bazaar is the place to buy almost anything in Istanbul.

When you find something you want to buy, ask the shopkeeper how much it costs, and then offer around half of what you're prepared to pay. The owner will feign amazement at such an insultingly low price, and discourse at length on the quality of the work, but will eventually suggest a lower price. You, of course, will plead poverty and suggest that you can buy the same thing more cheaply elsewhere, but end up making an offer slightly higher than your first. Ideally, you should have a partner who acts impatient and tries to get you to leave. This good-natured banter will continue back and forth until you settle on a mutually acceptable price. For expensive items, say a carpet or a leather jacket, the process might be lengthy and involve several glasses of tea and a good half hour of your time. Two golden rules: never begin bargaining for something you do not really intend to buy, and never quote a price that you aren't prepared to pay.

In the resorts on the coast, many traders are aware that some tourists feel uncomfortable with bargaining, and will give you their "best price" straight away if you ask them to. This is the minimum they are prepared to accept, and you will probably be wasting your time if you try to force them any lower. The competition between shops is fierce, and many traders work on very narrow profit margins.

What to Buy

Antiques. In a place steeped in history, buying antiques seems the logical thing to do. But remember, it is illegal to take genuine antiques out of the country without an export licence. If you want to buy any object that might be considered a museum piece, you will have to obtain a certificate from the directorate of a local museum that clears it for export. Despite this there are many interesting and attractive fake "antiques" for sale in Istanbul, including swords and daggers, Ottoman coffee-making sets, and copper and brass tray tables with wooden stands. But even if your purchase only *looks* "antique," it may still arouse suspicion at customs. Make sure the dealer gives you a *fatura* (invoice) stating the value of the piece, and when and where it was made.

Carpets and kilims. Turkish carpets are, of course, world famous for their beauty and durability, and are top of the shopping list for many visitors. *Kilims* are small rugs that are woven rather than knotted, and have no pile; a *cicim* is a kilim with embroidered decoration. All originated as floor and wall coverings for nomad dwellings—carpets as hard-wearing, insulated floor coverings, and kilims as covers and wall hangings. No two hand-made carpets are identical. The traditional patterns and symbols are handed down from generation to generation and have great significance to the weaver, conferring good luck on the household, protection against the "evil eye," or expressing the desire for a child. Ask the dealer to explain the symbols on any carpet you are thinking of buying.

The price of a carpet is affected by its age, rarity, quality of materials and dyes, and tightness of weave. The number of knots per square centimetre ranges from 20–30 for a coarse wool carpet to 100–200 for the most expensive silk carpets, which can cost tens of thousands of pounds. Natural dyes look better and last longer than synthetics, but are more expensive. You can tell the difference by wetting a corner of a white handkerchief and rubbing the carpet. Synthetic dyes will stain the white material, while the smell of chlorine means that the carpet has been bleached to make it look older. Even if you are not an expert, asking a few pertinent questions will make the carpet seller less likely to fob you off with an inferior item. Again, it is well worth doing your homework and shopping around a bit before deciding on which carpet to buy.

Ceramics and pottery. The best ceramic tiles ever produced in Turkey came from the kilns of İznik, near Bursa, but these are now collector's items. Today you will have to settle for polychrome tiles, bowls, plates, and vases made in Kütahya, which often copy the İznik designs but serve as affordable souvenirs.

Copper and brassware. Shining, hand-beaten objects in copper and brass can be found in the shops around the Old Bedesten in the Grand Bazaar, and also in Bakırcılar Caddesi (Coppersmiths' Street) behind Beyazıt Square. Braziers and shoeshine boxes, lamps, candlesticks, coffee-grinders, coffee-pots, and *samovars* are among the many objects available. The coppersmith will also be happy to make items to order, or to engrave your purchase. If you plan to use a copper item for boiling water or cooking, make sure that it is tinned on the inside, as unlined copper can be slightly toxic.

Leather and suede. Istanbul's Grand Bazaar has many leather shops offering a huge selection of handbags, belts, purses, wallets, jackets, trousers, and skirts. Prices and quality vary widely, but are generally about a half to two-thirds of what you would pay back home. While the leather is generally of good quality, some of the goods on offer in the popular tourist resorts suffer from poor stitching, so check the standard of craftsmanship carefully before buying. If you prefer you can have clothes and shoes made to order at many shops, but good-quality work will take time.

Jewellery. The best place to shop for quality jewellery is the Old Bedesten in the Grand Bazaar; cheaper items can be found in the shops along nearby Kalpakcılar Başı Caddesi (the bazaar's main street). Gold is sold by weight, with a surcharge for workmanship (gold prices are posted daily in the bazaar); genuine sterling silver should carry a hallmark. There are many cheap imitations on the market, with fake stones and silver plating, so beware of rip-offs, especially in the coastal resorts.

Other items you might consider include **nargiles,** the famous "hubble-bubble" pipes popular with old men in Turkish cafés; **meerschaum** pipes and figurines, produced in Eskişehir; luxurious Turkish **towels,** the best of which

Hand-crafted copper and brass items are staples of Turkish metalware.

A busy sidestreet alley branches off from the Grand Bazaar.

come from Bursa; colourful **Karagöz puppets,** made from dyed camel-hide; Muslim **prayerbeads** (*tespih*); traditional Turkish **musical instruments,** such as the mandolin-like *saz,* the *davul* (drum), or the *ney,* a Dervish flute; and **lokum,** better known as Turkish Delight, which comes in many flavours and can be found in shops in and around the Spice Bazaar. At Kuşadası, Bodrum, and Marmaris you'll see sponges in all shapes and sizes, while Bodrum's hand-crafted leather sandals are not only chic and cool, but practical, too.

ENTERTAINMENT

Nightlife

The Turkish-style supper clubs called *gazinos* offer an evening of folk music and belly-dancing, usually with dinner and drinks included. Most organized tours generally include a night at a *gazino* as part of the package; otherwise you can book a table through your hotel or through a travel agent. Many of the clubs are in Taksim and on the European shore of the Bosphorus; one of the best-known is at the top of the Galata Tower.

Western-style bars, discos, and nightclubs can be found in the Taksim district, but be warned that the clubs in the side streets off İstiklal Caddesi are mostly rip-off joints where you will be charged an enormous bill for a round of drinks, and forcibly relieved of your wallet if you refuse to pay up. There are also good bars in Ataköy (southwest of the city), and in Ortaköy and Bebek on the Bosphorus.

Music and Cinema

The Atatürk Cultural Centre on Taksim Square offers a programme of opera, ballet, and symphony concerts from October to May; during the Istanbul International Festival, held from mid-June to mid-July), the city hosts musicians and performers from all over the world. Jazz is popular in Istanbul, and many bars and clubs have live bands performing over the weekends.

There are many cinemas in İstiklal Caddesi, and a multi-screen theatre at Çemberlitaş in the Old City, which show mainstream movies. Look for the word *orijinal* on

---

Calendar of Events/Festivals

Exact dates should be confirmed through local tourist offices.

January *Selçuk:* Camel-wrestling Festival.

April–May *Istanbul/Kuşadası/Selçuk:* Istanbul International Film Festival—new releases of Turkish and foreign films.

June *Bergama:* Bergama Festival. *Bursa:* International Bursa Festival. *Foça, near İzmir:* Ephesus International Festival of Culture and Tourism.

June–July *Çeşme:* Sea and Music Festival. *Istanbul:* Istanbul International Arts Festival.

August–September *İzmir:* İzmir International Fair.

October *Bodrum:* International Bodrum Cup—Yacht Races.

the poster—this means that the film will be shown in its original language, with Turkish subtitles; otherwise it has been dubbed.

Sound and Light Show

From June to September you can enjoy a free sound-and-light show at the Blue Mosque (the viewing benches are about halfway between the mosque and Haghia Sophia). The show, which begins each evening at 9:00 P.M., relates in melodramatic fashion the history of Istanbul while coloured floodlights illuminate the spectacular architecture of the Blue Mosque. The commentary is in English, French, German, or Turkish, in rotation—check the notice by the benches for the date of the next performance in English.

Turkish Baths

No trip to Turkey would be complete without a visit to the *hamam*, or Turkish bath. There are a couple of historic baths in Istanbul which cater specifically for tourists, namely the 18th-century Çağaloğlu Hamamı in Sultanah-

Belly Dancing

This ancient art is thought to have its origins in Africa. It is a popular entertainment for locals as well as tourists, and the best dancers are famous, often appearing on TV.

A belly dance is not just a performance, it's an invitation to join in—any Turkish gent worth his salt will be up shimmying on the dance floor at the earliest opportunity. Even if you don't join in, you can show your appreciation by moistening a bank-note and sticking it on the dancer's forehead, or—despite principles of equality—tucking it into her bra or waistband.

met, and 16th-century Galatasaray Hamamı in Beyoğlu. These places are worth a visit for their interior marble architecture alone, but the opportunity to experience a genuine Turkish bath should not be missed. There are usually separate entrances for men (*erkek*) and women (*kadın*), but if there is only one chamber, then different times are set aside for men and women.

The ancient art of belly dancing is open to onlookers who wish to join in on the fun.

Leave your valuables in a locker at the desk and get undressed in the changing room. Wearing a towel and bath-clogs, you will be shown to the steamy marble washroom, where buckets of hot water will be poured over you before an attendant sets to work with a coarse glove, removing dirt and dead skin and leaving you pink and glowing. You can also have a massage at this point (for an additional fee). Afterwards you retire to the changing room for tea or a drink, feeling completely relaxed and rejuvenated.

SPORTS

Watersports

The Aegean coast is a watersports paradise, but pollution around Istanbul means that you will have to travel some distance from the city in order to enjoy clean water. The best beaches within easy reach of the city are the attractive Black Sea resorts of **Kilyos** and **Şile.** In summer, a bus leaves Üsküdar for Şile every hour from 9:00 A.M. for the two-hour journey. To get to Kilyos, take a ferry or bus to Sarıyer, where a taxi or *dolmuş* (see page 125) will take you the 12 km (7½ miles) to the coast. There are good swimming beaches on the **Princes' Islands,** too, but they get extremely crowded at weekends. West of the city, there are beaches at Florya (20 km/12½ miles), and farther out at Silivri and Gümüşyaka (65 km/40 miles).

All the standard beach sports can be enjoyed at the main Aegean resorts—windsurfing, water-skiing, parasailing, and jet-skiing. Equipment hire and instruction are available for those who want it. There is a major wind-surfing and dinghy-sailing school at Bitez, near Bodrum.

Sailing is just one aspect of the watersports paradise that surrounds Istanbul.

Skiing

Uludağ (Great Mountain, with a height of 1,800 metres/5,400 feet), above Bursa, is Turkey's largest ski resort, with a season lasting from December to March. A cable-car (*teleferik*) links Bursa directly to the ski area; alternatively, you can drive 36 km (22 miles) up a winding mountain road to the hotel zone. There are a dozen or so hotels, which are usually booked solid at weekends in winter; they can hire out equipment if needed. Each hotel has its own ski-tow—there is no comprehensive ski-pass system. The slopes may not be very challenging, but there's enough to keep you interested for a few days.

Spectator Sports

Unique to Turkey is the national sport of **oiled wrestling** (*yağlı güreş*). An annual gathering is held in June at Kırkpınar, near Edirne, 230 km (143 miles) northwest of Istanbul. The competitors, wearing only a pair of leather breeches, coat themselves in olive oil and perform a ceremonial procession before getting to grips with their slippery opponents and flinging each other around to the delighted cheers of thousands of spectators.

An even more exotic spectacle is **camel wrestling** (*deve güreşi*), which can be seen in January at Selçuk, near Kuşadası. These hump-backed beasts are bad-tempered, and when two moody males confront each other in the ring a fierce sparring match ensues, in which they use their necks to try to throw each other off balance. Before they get injured they are separated, and the winner is decided by a panel of judges while the loser is dragged off.

After that scene, **horse racing** may seem rather tame by comparison. Races are held between April and December at the Veliefendi Hippodrome near Bakırköy, 15 km (9 miles) west of Istanbul. In winter, they move to İzmir.

EATING OUT

Turkey has one of the world's richest cuisines, with influences derived from the many cultures of the former Ottoman Empire, and top-quality produce from Anatolia's lush farmland and fertile seas. Many dishes originated in the kitchens of the Ottoman sultans—in the time of Süleyman the Magnificent there were more than 150 recipes for aubergines alone. Most tourists, however, will be exposed to only a small range of Turkish dishes, unless they are invited into a Turkish home, or eat at one of the country's better restaurants. The majority of eating places in Istanbul and the Aegean resorts offer the standard fare of bread, salads, kebabs, and seafood.

Meal Times

The typical Turkish breakfast, served between 7:00 and 10:00 A.M., usually consists of fresh bread, butter, and jam, with olives cucumber, tomato, white cheese, and perhaps a hard-boiled egg, washed down with sweet black tea. Try asking for *menemen*, a delicious dish of eggs scrambled with tomatoes, green peppers, and onion.

In Turkey, people eat out regularly, and as a result there are many restaurants, cafés, and food stalls open all day and late into the evening. There are no set times for lunch and dinner, especially in tourist areas, and you can eat at almost any time of day.

A typical Turkish meal begins with a spread of *meze* (starters), washed down with *rakı*, followed by grilled meat, fish, or kebabs, and rounded off with fresh fruit or milk puddings, and cups of the famous strong black Turkish coffee.

When ordering, it is customary to be taken to the kitchen to look at the various dishes—you will find printed menus only in tourist restaurants. Don't order a main course until you have finished the *meze*; you may be too full to appreciate it. It is perfectly acceptable to have a meal composed entirely of *meze*.

Where to Eat

Many of the eating places in Turkey specialize in serving a certain kind of dish. An average restaurant, offering a variety of typically Turkish food and drink, freshly prepared, is called a *lokanta* or *restoran*, and may or may not be licensed. A *gazino* is a restaurant that serves alcohol, and usually also offers an evening floor show of belly-dancing and folk music. *Hazır yemek* ("ready food") means that you can choose your meal from heated trays of pre-cooked food.

A *kebapçı* specializes in grilled meats, notably kebabs served with *pide* and salad, while a *pideci* or *pide salonu* is a Turkish-style pizza parlour, dishing up tasty *pide* (unleavened bread) topped with minced lamb, eggs, or cheese. You can enjoy lamb meatballs in a *köfteci*, tripe in an *işkembeci*, soup in a *çorbacı*, and milk puddings in a *muhallebici*. A *büfe* is a street kiosk which sells snacks and soft-drinks. (See recommended restaurants on pages 137–143.)

What to Eat

Starters (meze)

Meze is the collective name given to a wide selection of appetizers, both hot and cold. They are usually pre-

The fish market by Galata Bridge provides seafood for local restaurants.

sented on a tray at your table, or in a glass-fronted display case, and you can choose as few or as many dishes as you like. The more popular offerings include *kuru fasulye* (haricot beans in tomato sauce), *patlıcan kızartması* (aubergine fried in olive oil and garlic), *şakşuka* (aubergine, tomato, and hot peppers in oil), *cacık* (yoghurt with cucumber and garlic), *biber dolması* (green peppers stuffed with rice, raisins, and pine nuts), *sigara böreği* (cheese-filled pastry rolls), and a range of salads. *Çerkez tavuğu* (Circassian chicken) is a classic dish of chicken fillet cooked in a sauce flavoured with ground walnuts and paprika. *Meze* are served with fresh white bread to soak up the oil and juices.

Soups (çorba)

Turkish soups are usually thick and substantial. Try *düğün çorbası* ("wedding" soup, a mutton broth flavoured with lemon juice and cayenne, and thickened with egg), *mercimek çorbası* (red lentil soup), or *işkembe çorbası* (tripe soup, believed to be a hangover cure). *İşkembecis* stay open until the early hours of the morning to serve bowls of tripe soup to peckish late-night revellers on their way home.

Main Courses

Ask anyone to name a typically Turkish dish and the likely answer you'll get is *kebap*—the well-known grilled, broiled, or roasted meat. The most common varieties are *şiş kebap* (cubes of lamb threaded on a skewer and grilled over charcoal); *döner kebap* (literally "revolving" kebap—a stack of marinated, sliced lamb and minced mutton roasted on a vertical spit, with slices cut off as the outer layers cook); *Adana kebap* (spicy minced beef moulded around a skewer and grilled); and *fırın kebap* (oven-roasted fillet of lamb marinated in yoghurt).

The ubiquitous *İskender kebap* is a dish of *döner kebap* served on a bed of diced *pide* bread with tomato sauce and yoghurt, topped with a sizzling splash of browned butter. *Çiftlik kebap* is a casserole of lamb, onion, and peas. Meatballs of minced lamb, usually served with a tomato sauce, are called *köfte*. A classic Turkish dish, well worth asking for, is *mantarlı güveç*, a delicious stew of tender lamb, mushrooms, peppers, tomatoes, and garlic baked in a clay dish and topped with cheese.

Waterfront dining is a great way to enjoy the sunset.

Seafood

The seas around Turkey abound with fish, and waterfront restaurants serve up the catch of the day, sold by weight. Choose your own fish from the display and find out how much it will cost before having it cooked. Some of the tastiest species are *levrek* (sea bass), *barbunya* (red mullet), *palamut* (bonito), *uskumru* (mackerel), and *lüfer* (bluefish). The best way to enjoy your fish is simply to have it grilled over charcoal; the waiter will remove the bones if you ask. Look out for *kılıç şiş*, chunks of juicy swordfish skewered with onion, pepper, and tomato, and grilled.

Other kinds of seafood more commonly appear as *meze*— *kalamar* (squid), *ahtapod* (octopus), *karides* (prawns), *sardalya* (sardines), and *midye* (mussels). The mussels are either coated in flour and fried (*midye tava*), or stuffed with

Tea is the Turkish national drink, usually served in tulip-shaped glasses.

rice, pine nuts, raisins, and cinnamon (*midye dolması*).

Desserts

Fresh fruit is often served to round off a meal—succulent *karpuz* (watermelon) and *kavun* (musk melon), *kiraz* (cherries), *kayısı* (apricot), *incir* (figs), *düt* (mulberries), and *erik* (sour plums)—but when it comes to prepared desserts, the Turks have a very sweet tooth. The most well known is *lokum* (Turkish Delight), a soft jelly, flavoured with rosewater and sprinkled with icing sugar. Another classic dessert is *baklava,* made of alternating layers of thin pastry and ground pistachios, almonds, or walnuts, saturated with syrup. Many other sugary confections have names which betray their origins in the harem—*dilber dudağı* ("lips of the beloved"), *hanım göbeği* ("lady's navel"), and *bülbül yuvası* ("nightingale's nest").

A traditional Turkish pudding shop (*muhallebici*) serves milk- and rice-based desserts like *fırın sütlaç* (baked rice pudding), *zerde* (a saffron-flavoured rice pudding), and *tavuk göğsü* (a combination of rice, milk, sugar, and chicken breast). A more unusual dish is *aşure*, a kind of sweet porridge made with cereals, nuts, and fruit sprinkled with rose water.

Drinks

The Turkish national drink is **tea** (*çay*). It is drunk throughout the day, in shops, cafés, and offices, oiling the wheels of commerce, and sealing many a business deal. If you bargain for a carpet in the Grand Bazaar you will get through two or three glasses of *çay* before a price is agreed. Tea is usually served black in small tulip-shaped glasses.

Turkish coffee (*kahve*) is strong, black, and served complete with grounds in a small espresso cup, with a glass of water on the side. Sugar is added while brewing, so order *sade kahve* (no sugar), *orta kahve* (sweet), or *çok şekerli kahve* (very sweet). Leave it for a moment for the grounds to settle, and remember not to drain your cup. If you want instant coffee, ask for Nescafé.

You should avoid drinking tap **water,** and stick to bottled mineral water, which is easily available everywhere —*maden suyu* is carbonated mineral water, *memba suyu* is still mineral water. A traditional Turkish thirst-quencher is *ayran*, a 50–50 mixture of yoghurt and mineral water, seasoned with a pinch of salt.

The national alcoholic drink is a very potent anise liquor called *rakı*. It is drunk as an aperitif, and indeed throughout the meal. It should be mixed half-and-half with iced water, with a glass of water on the side (when mixed with water it turns a pearly white, hence its nickname, *aslan sütü* — lion's milk). Turkish-made beer is also a popular thirst-quencher, and of good quality.

Turkish **wines** (*şarap*) have a history going back as far as 7000 B.C., and some believe that European vine-stocks may well have originated here. Despite good quality local wines, the Turks are not great wine drinkers. Only a small proportion of the harvest goes into wine-making; they prefer beer and *rakı*. You can choose from a wide range of Turkish reds, whites, rosés, and sparkling wines at very reasonable prices. Names to look out for include Villa Doluca, Çankaya, Kavak, and Dikmen.

INDEX

HANDY TRAVEL TIPS

An A–Z Summary of Practical Information

A

ACCOMMODATION *(oteller)* (See also CAMPING, YOUTH HOSTELS, and the list of RECOMMENDED HOTELS starting on page 129)

Despite increased hotel prices, Istanbul can still be a bargain for the independent traveller. The luxury accommodation is concentrated around Taksim Square, while middle-range hotels cluster amid the warren of back streets in Laleli and Aksaray; the cheapest hotels and pensions, many of them very pleasant, can be found between Sultanahmet and Sirkeci.

One-star hotels provide clean, basic rooms, though most do offer private bathrooms. At the 3-star level, you can begin looking for air-conditioning and TV. Five-star hotels are on a par with similar establishments around the world, and so are their prices. Advance booking is not normally required for the lower- and middle-range hotels, but is for the more sought-after ones.

By law, room rates must be displayed in reception and in the rooms. The quoted rates usually include VAT (KDV in Turkish) at 15%, and breakfast. If the hotel is not full, do not be afraid to "discuss" a lower price.

A list of hotels officially rated by the Turkish Ministry of Tourism is available from their overseas representative offices (see TOURIST INFORMATION OFFICES).

Accommodation tips

- Consider paying a little extra for an air-conditioned room in July and August.
- Take a plug for the bath and basin; you'll rarely find one in hotels, since Muslims wash in running water.
- If you're intending to stay in cheap pensions, travel with soap, towel, and toilet paper—rarely are all three present at once.
- Solar-powered water heaters are common, so you're more likely to have hot water in the evening than in the morning.

Istanbul

- Breakfast is usually optional and, aside from swanky hotels' buffets, dull; rather, decline, and buy snacks sold on the street instead.
- Some smarter hotels insist on half-board arrangements, which are best avoided; local restaurants generally serve better food.
- When checking in, it's common practice to ask to see a room first. Always bargain: prices displayed are maximum rates.

I'd like a single/double room.	**Tek/çift yataklı bir oda istiyorum.**
What's the rate per night?	**Bir gecelik oda ücreti ne kadar?**

AIRPORT *(havalimanı; havaalanı)*

Istanbul is served by Atatürk International Airport (*Atatürk Havalimanı*), 24 km (15 miles) to the south west of the city. The international (*dışhatları*) and domestic (*içhatları*) terminals are linked by a free shuttle bus; journey time is about five minutes. Stops are not well-signposted, however, so you must ask.

The airport offers a currency exchange, bank, post office, car rental, tourist information desk, restaurants and duty-free shops. A bus service called Havaş runs between the airport and the city centre, with services hourly between 6am and 11pm, half-hourly from 2 until 6pm. Journey time is around 30 minutes, though the trip can take much longer during rush hours. Buses depart from the far side of the car-park outside the arrivals hall and stop at Aksaray in the old city, and Sişhane near Taksim Square.

Taxis are faster and more convenient than the bus, taking only 20 to 30 minutes to the city centre.

B

BUDGETING FOR YOUR TRIP

In general, accommodation and meals cost less in Turkey than they do in Western Europe. Expect to pay from between $35 (about

£20) and up for decent accommodation, and $10 (or £6) for a decent meal, including wine. The cost of public transportation is minimal: (about 16¢, or 10p) for buses, and taxis are also inexpensive, at about $4.50, or £3, from Sultanhamet to Taksim.

C

CAMPING *(kamping)*

The nearest, easily accessible campsite to the centre of Istanbul is the *Ataköy Tatil Köyü* (Ataköy Holiday Village), 16 km (10 miles) from the city centre and 8 km (5 miles) from the airport. The site has a swimming pool, bar and disco. For reservations, tel. (212) 559-6000.

Is there a campsite nearby?	**Yakında kamping veri var mı?**
Can we camp here?	**Burada kamp yapabilir miyiz?**

CAR RENTAL *(araba kiralama)* (See also DRIVING)

A car is more of a liability than a luxury in traffic-packed Istanbul. However, if you plan to travel further afield, renting a car is a good way of getting around Turkey (especially since the rail system in Turkey is not extensive). Rates at the numerous car rental firms vary considerably—local firms often charge substantially less than the big international chains. You can get good rates by booking and paying for your car before you leave home, either directly through the U.K. office of an international rental company, or as part of a "fly-drive" package deal. Check that the quoted rate includes Collision Damage Waiver, unlimited mileage, and VAT (KDV in Turkey). Note that rental car insurance never covers you for broken windscreens and burst tyres. Unless you hire a four-wheel-drive car, you will not be insured for driving on unsurfaced roads.

Istanbul

You must be over 21 to rent, and you will need your passport, a valid driver's licence (EU model) held for at least 12 months, and a major credit card—cash deposits are prohibitively large.

I'd like to hire a car (tomorrow).	**Bir araba kiralamak stiyorum (yarın).**
for one day/a week	**bir gün/bir hafta için**
Please include full insurance.	**Lütfen, sigortası da tam olsun.**

CLIMATE and CLOTHING

Climate. Istanbul enjoys a typically Mediterranean, temperate climate with warm, dry summers and cool, wet winters. July and August are the hottest months. The prevailing wind, the *poyraz*, blows down the Bosphorus from the northeast, and provides a welcome cooling breeze, but when the wind drops it can become uncomfortably humid, with occasional thunderstorms. The southwest wind, called the *lodos*, usually brings storms on the Sea of Marmara. The best time to visit the city is in April, May, and June when the days are pleasantly warm, and the shores of the Bosphorus are bright with spring flowers and the blossoms of judas trees. Winter is generally cold, wet, and uncomfortable. Snow is not uncommon in midwinter, though it rarely settles for more than a few days.

The table below shows the average daily maximum and minimum temperatures for Istanbul:

	J	F	M	A	M	J	J	A	S	O	N	D
°C Max	8	9	11	16	21	25	28	28	24	20	15	11
°C min	3	2	3	7	12	16	18	19	16	13	9	5
°F max	46	47	51	60	69	77	82	82	76	68	59	51
°F min	37	36	38	45	53	60	65	66	61	55	48	41

Clothing. When it's hot, lightweight cotton clothes are the most comfortable choice, but evenings sometimes turn cool, especially in spring and autumn, so take along a jacket or sweater. Also take a long-sleeved shirt and sun hat to protect against the midday sun. In winter, warm clothes and a raincoat or umbrella will be needed.

Respectable clothing should, of course, be worn when visiting mosques and other Islamic monuments—long trousers or skirt, a long-sleeved shirt or blouse, and a headscarf for women. At the Blue Mosque, robes are provided for unsuitably attired tourists.

COMMUNICATIONS (See also TIME DIFFERENCES)

Post Offices (*postane*). Post offices handle mail, parcels, telegrams and telephone calls, and often currency exchange as well; they are marked by a yellow sign with the letters "PTT." If you want to buy stamps, look for the counter marked "*pul.*" Hours are 8:30am-8pm for postal services, until midnight for telephone and telegrams.

The main post office in Istanbul is in Yeni Postane Sokak (turn left, facing the ferries, at the Sirkeci tram stop); other branches are in the Grand Bazaar and at Galatasaray Square. Stamps can also be bought at tourist shops selling postcards. Post boxes are scarce—post your mail at your hotel desk, or at a PTT office. There are usually three slots—marked *şehiriçi* for local addresses; *yurtiçi* for destinations within Turkey; and *yurtdışı* for international mail.

Poste restante (general delivery). If you don't know ahead of time where you will be staying, you can have your mail addressed to you ^c/o Poste Restante, with your surname underlined, eg: Mr. John <u>Smith</u>, Poste Restante, Büyük PTT, Yeni Postane Sokak, Sirkeci, Istanbul, Turkey. It will be held for you at the main post office; take your passport along as identification.

Telephones (*telefon*). You can make domestic and international telephone calls from public telephones at PTT offices, or telephone boxes on the street. These accept either telephone cards (*telekart*) or a metal token called a *jeton*. Cards and *jetons* can be bought at the PTT, and at some news-stands and kiosks. To make a local call, lift the receiver, insert your card or tokens, and dial the seven-digit number. For intercity calls (including calls to Üsküdar across the Bosphorus), dial 0, then the area code, then the number. The ringing tone is a single long tone.

Istanbul

To make an international call, dial 00 and wait for a second tone, then dial the country code (44 for the U.K., 353 for Ireland, 1 for the U.S.A. and Canada), and the full number including area code.

Have you received any mail for me?	**Bana posta var mı acaba?**
A stamp for this letter/postcard, please	**Bu mektup/kart için bir pul, lütfen.**
express (special delivery)	**ekspres**
airmail	**uçak ile**
registered	**taahütlü**
I want to send a telegram to…	**…(ya) bir telgraf yollamak istiyorum.**
reverse-charge (collect) call	**ödemeli**
person-to-person (personal) call	**ihbarlı**

COMPLAINTS (*şikayet*)

Complaints should first be made to the management of the hotel, restaurant or shop. If you're still not satisfied, then go to the tourist information office (see TOURIST INFORMATION OFFICES). To avoid problems, always establish a price in advance.

CRIME (See also EMERGENCIES and POLICE)

You are far less likely to be a victim of crime in Turkey than you are in Western Europe and North America. Nevertheless, you should take the usual precautions against theft. In order to comply with your travel insurance, report any theft or loss to the police. If your passport is lost or stolen, you should also inform your consulate. Remember that drug use or trafficking is punishable by severe prison sentences.

CUSTOMS and ENTRY FORMALITIES

Visas. U.K., U.S., and Irish citizens will need a full passport. and require a visa that can be purchased from the visa desk before going through passport control in Turkey. The cost is U.S. $45, or £28, or the equivalent in Turkish lire. (Visa regulations do change, and should be checked through your travel agent.)

Currency restrictions. There is no limit on the amount of foreign currency that may be brought in, but no more than US$5,000 worth of Turkish *lira* can be brought in or taken out of the country. However, remember that, due to inflation, the Turkish *lira* loses value rapidly and is hard to exchange outside the country.

Visitors to Turkey are allowed to bring in 200 cigarettes and 50 cigars and 200g tobacco plus 0.5l spirits or 0.5l wine. In addition to these allowances you may bring up to 400 cigarettes, 100 cigars and 500g of tobacco from a Turkish duty-free shop when you arrive.

Into:	Cigarettes		Cigars		Tobacco	Spirits		Wine
Canada	200	and	50	and	900g	1.1l	or	1l
U.K. and Ireland	200	or	50	or	250g	1 l	and	2 l
U.S.A.	200	and	100	and	*	1 l	and	2 l

*a reasonable quantity

Antiquities. Buying and exporting antiquities is strictly forbidden. If you buy any object which might be classified as an antiquity (e.g.; antiques, old coins, and even old carpets), make sure that it is from a reputable dealer, who will be able to provide you with an invoice (*fatura*) stating its value. "Roman" coins and figurines sold by boys at archaeological sites are mostly worthless fakes.

D

DRIVING in ISTANBUL (See also CAR RENTAL, EMERGENCIES)

If you bring your own vehicle, you will need a full driver's licence, an International Motor Insurance Certificate, and "Green Card" (make sure it's valid for the Asian sector if you plan to cross the Dardanelles or Bosphorus), and a Vehicle Registration Document. An official nationality plate must be displayed near the rear number plate, and headlamp beams must be adjusted if necessary for driving on the right. Motoring organizations have full details on requirements for Turkey and other countries that you may be driving through en route..

Wearing seat belts in both front and back seats is obligatory; on-the-spot fines can be issued for non-compliance. A red warning triangle and a fire extinguisher must be carried. Motorcycle riders and their passengers must wear crash helmets. Note that the minimum legal age for driving in Turkey is 18 years old, and that laws prohibiting drinking and driving are strictly enforced.

Rules of the road. Drive on the right, and pass on the left. Speed limits are 130 km/h (80 mph) on motorways, 90 km/h (55 mph) on highways, and 40 or 50 km/h (25 or 30 mph) in towns and cities. Traffic joining a road from the right has priority, unless signs or markings indicate otherwise.

There are new toll motorways between Istanbul, Edirne, and Ankara and around İzmir, which are fast to travel on, and often nearly deserted.

Fuel. In western Turkey, there are plenty of petrol (gas) stations, and many are open 24 hours a day. However, there are as yet very few service stations on the toll motorways. Most of the rental cars run on *normal* (also called *benzin*); premium grade petrol is called *super*, and diesel is *motorin*. Lead-free petrol (*kurşunsuz*) is still not widespread, but can be found in and around Istanbul and İzmir.

Parking. Watch out for signs saying *park yapİlmaz* or *park yasaktır* (no parking)— the local police enforce parking regulations rigidly, and will tow away any illegally parked vehicles within a very short time. You will have to pay a fine to retrieve your car from the pound. The best bet is to look for an official car park (*otopark*).

Traffic police. You can recognize the Turkish *Trafik Polisi* by their black-and-white baseball-style caps and two-tone Renault patrol cars. They patrol city streets and highways, and have the power to issue on-the-spot fines for traffic offences.

Breakdown. Most towns have a mechanic. Larger towns and cities have full repair shops and towing services. For rental cars, there will usually be a 24-hour emergency telephone number, and the company will arrange for repairs or a replacement. For tyre repairs, look for a sign saying *lastikçi*, usually painted on an old tyre at the roadside.

Road signs. Main roads are well signposted; sights of interest to tourists are marked by special yellow signs with black lettering. Below are some common Turkish signs:

DİKKAT	caution
DUR	stop
GİRİLMEZ	no entry
PARK YAPILMAZ	no parking
ŞEHİR MERKEZİ	town centre
TEK YÖN	one way
TİRMANMA ŞERİDİ	overtaking lane
YAVAŞ	slow
YOL VER	give way
YOL YAPIMI	road works
24 SAAT AÇIK	open 24 hours
(International) Driving Permit	**(uluslararası) ehliyet**

Istanbul

car registration papers	**araba ruhsatı**
Green Card	**yeşil kartı**
Can I park here?	**Buraya park edebilir miyim?**
Are we on the right road for…?	**…için doğru yolda mıyız?**
Full tank, please.	**Dodurun, lütfen.**
I've broken down.	**Arabam arzalandı.**
There's been an accident.	**Bir kaza oldu.**

E

ELECTRIC CURRENT

220-volt, 50-cycle is standard. An adapter for Continental-style two-pin sockets will be needed; American 110-volt appliances will also require a transformer.

I need an adapter/a battery.   **Bir adaptör/pil istiyorum.**

EMBASSIES and CONSULATES *(elçilik; konsolosluk)*

Embassies are in the capital city of Ankara.

British Consulate:	Meşrutiyet Caddesi 34, Tepebaşı, Beyoğlu, Istanbul; tel. (212) 293-7545.
Irish Consulate:	Cumhuriyet Caddesi 26A, Elmadağ, Istanbul; tel. (212) 246-6025.
US Consulate:	Meşrutiyet Caddesi 104-8, Tepebaşı, Beyoğlu, Istanbul; tel. (212) 251-3602.

EMERGENCIES

You will need a *jeton* or phonecard to call these numbers from a public telephone.

Police	**155**
Ambulance	**112**
Fire	**110**

ETIQUETTE

The Turks are by nature friendly, courteous, and immensely hospitable—do not allow the persistent carpet-shop hustlers in places like Istanbul's Grand Bazaar to influence your opinion of them.

Most important of all is dress. You will notice that the people of Istanbul dress modestly, and avoid shorts and skimpy tops even in the heat of summer. When visiting mosques wear long trousers or a skirt reaching below the knee, with a long-sleeved shirt or blouse. Women should cover their heads with a scarf. At the Blue Mosque, scantily clad tourists are given robes to wear while visiting the mosque's interior. Mosques are open to tourists except during prayer times especially on Fridays, the Moslem holy day. Take your shoes off before entering a mosque or a Turkish house or apartment.

You should never make jokes or insulting comments about Atatürk or the Turkish flag, or behave disrespectfully towards them (ie., don't climb on a statue of Atatürk to have your photo taken).

Body language can be confusing. If someone shakes their head, that means "I don't understand." "No" is indicated by tilting your head back while raising your eyebrows, such as a Westerner might do to say, "Pardon me? I didn't catch what you said."

GUIDES *(rehber)* and TOURS

Official, English-speaking guides can be hired through the local tourist office (see TOURIST INFORMATION OFFICES) and also through travel agencies and the better hotels. They are usually friendly and knowledgeable, and can prove invaluable if your time is limited. Freelance guides also hang around at the entrance to Topkapı Palace (make sure you agree on a price before hiring one).

We'd like an English-speaking guide. **İngilizce bilen bir rehber istiyoruz.**

Istanbul

I need an English interpreter. **İngilizce bilen bir çevirmene ihtiyacım var.**

L

LANGUAGE

In the main tourist destinations many people are fluent in English, and many more speak a little. Locals will welcome any attempt you make to speak their language. The Berlitz TURKISH PHRASE BOOK AND DICTIONARY will cover most situations you are likely to encounter there. (See also the inside front cover of this guide for some expressions.) Below is the pronunciation of some Turkish letters:

c like **j** in **j**am
ç like **ch** in **ch**ip
ğ almost silent; lengthens the preceding vowel
h always clearly pronounced
ı like **i** in s**i**r
j like **s** in plea**s**ure
ö approx. like **ur** in f**ur** (like German *ö*)
ş like **sh** in **sh**ell
ü approx. like **ew** in f**ew** (like German *ü*)

Numbers

0	**sıfır**	13	**onüç**	50	**elli**
1	**bir**	14	**ondört**	60	**altmış**
2	**iki**	15	**onbeş**	70	**yetmiş**
3	**üç**	16	**onaltı**	80	**seksen**
4	**dürt**	17	**onyedi**	90	**doksan**
5	**beş**	18	**onsekiz**	100	**yüz**
6	**altı**	19	**ondokuz**	101	**yüzbir**
7	**yedi**	20	**yirmi**	126	**yüzyirmi altı**
8	**sekiz**	21	**yirmibir**	200	**ikiyüz**
9	**dokuz**	22	**yirmiiki**	300	**üçyüz**
10	**on**	23	**yirmiüç**	1,000	**bin**
11	**onbir**	30	**otuz**	2,500	**ikibinbeşyüz**
12	**oniki**	40	**kırk**	10,000	**on bin**

LAUNDRY *(çamaşır)*

Your hotel will be able to provide a laundry service, even if you are staying in a modest one-star establishment; usually, washing must be handed in before noon for return the following morning. There are very few coin-operated launderettes. In Istanbul, try Active Laundry, Emin Paşa Sokak 14, off Divan Yolu, in the Sultanahmet district.

LOST PROPERTY *(kayıp eşya)* (See also CRIME)

Ask for advice from your hotel receptionist or the local Tourist Information Office (see page 124) before contacting the police. For items left behind on public transport, ask your hotel receptionist to telephone the bus or train station or taxi company.

I've lost my wallet/handbag/ passport.	**Cüzdanımı/El çantamı/ Pasaportumu kaybettim.**

M

MEDIA

Television. The state-owned TRT (*Türkiye Radyo ve Televizyon*) broadcasts a number of nationwide TV channels. News in English is shown at 10:30pm on TRT-2, while international sporting events can be found on TRT-3. The better hotels have satellite TV, with BBC World Service, CNN, MTV, Superchannel, etc. is becoming increasingly common in hotels.

Radio. On shortwave radio you will get English BBC World Service and Voice of America. There are regular news summaries in English on TRT-3 (88.4, 94.0 and 99.0 MHz).

Newspapers. The English-language *Turkish Daily News* is published Monday to Saturday, and offers national and international news and features. You can buy British newspapers at several news-stands in Istanbul (in Sultanahmet, Laleli, and

Taksim) and in the main tourist resorts; they're usually a day
late, and rather expensive.

| Have you any English-language newspapers? | **Bir İngiliz gazeteniz var mı?** |

MEDICAL CARE

There is no free health care for visitors to Turkey. You should have
an adequate insurance policy, preferably one that includes cover for
an emergency flight home in the event of serious injury or illness.

The main health hazards in Turkey are the sun, and the risk of
diarrhoea. Take along a sun hat, sunglasses, and plenty of high-
factor sun-screen. Cover up or stay indoors during the middle of
the day, and limit your sun-bathing sessions to a half-hour or less.

To avoid diarrhoea eat only freshly cooked food, and drink only
bottled water and canned or bottled drinks (without ice). Avoid
restaurants that look dirty, food from street stalls, undercooked meat,
salads and fruit (except fruit you can peel yourself), dairy produce,
and tap water. Standards of hygiene are usually quite adequate.

For minor ailments, seek advice from the local pharmacy
(*eczane*), usually open during normal shopping hours. After hours,
at least one per town is open all night, called the *nöbet* or *nöbetci;*
its location is posted in the window of all other pharmacies.

Vaccinations. There are no compulsory immunization requirements for entry into Turkey. Up-to-date vaccinations for tetanus,
polio, typhoid, and hepatitis A are recommended, especially for
independent travellers who intend "roughing it" in rural areas. A
course of anti-malarial tablets is recommended for anyone plan-
ning to visit the Antalya region or the south east.

Where's the nearest pharmacy?	**En yakın eczane nerededir?**
Where can I find a doctor/ a dentist?	**Nereden bir doktor/bir dişci bulabilirim?**
an ambulance	**bir ambülans**
hospital	**hastane**

sunburn	**güneş yanığı**
sunstroke	**güneş çarptı**
a fever	**ateş**
an upset stomach	**mide bozulması**

MONEY MATTERS (See also CUSTOMS and ENTRY FORMALITIES)

Currency. The unit is the Turkish *lira* (TL). Notes come in denominations of 5,000, 10,000, 20,000, 50,000, 100,000, 250,000, 500,000, 1,000,000, and 5,000,000TL, and coins in 500, 1,000, 2,500, 5,000, 10,000, 25,000, and 50,000TL.

Banks and Currency Exchange (*banka*; *kambiyo*; *döviz*). Banks are generally open 8:30am-noon and 1:30-5pm Monday to Friday. The most efficient banks are the Türk Ticaret Bankası, the Yapı ve Kredi, and the AkBank. Rates of exchange and commission vary considerably, so it's worth shopping around. The rate in Turkey is always better than in the U.K. ATM machines, which administer *lira* drawn against your bank account, are commonplace.

In the more popular tourist resorts the banks have exchange booths which open independently of the main bank, often 8am-8pm including weekends. You will find the best exchange rates at the many independent currency dealers called *döviz*, which stay open late in the evening and at weekends, and are often crowded out with local people. They deal only in cash, not traveller's cheques. You can also change cash and traveller's cheques at the PTT office.

Traveller's cheques (*travelers çek*). Generally accepted by middle and upper grade hotels, and by the banks mentioned above. Smaller branches may refuse to cash them and will direct you elsewhere.

Credit cards (*kredi kartı*). Major credit and charge cards—Visa, Access/Mastercard, American Express, and Diners Club—are accepted in the more expensive hotels (3-star and above) and restaurants in the larger cities, and by tourist shops and car rental firms. Visa and Access/Mastercard can also be used in banks to obtain cash advances, and in automatic teller machines to withdraw cash (Turkish *lira* only). A credit card and an ATM is the fastest and easiest way of getting cash in Turkey, and is cheaper than using traveller's cheques.

I want to change some pounds/ dollars.	**Sterlin/Dolar bozdurmak istiyorum.**
Do you accept traveller's cheques?	**Seyahat çeki kabul eder misiniz?**
Can I pay with this credit card?	**Bu kredi kartımla ödeyebilir miyim?**

OPENING HOURS

Banks: 8:30am to noon and 1:30 to 5pm Monday to Friday.

Currency Exchange Offices: 8am to 8pm daily.

Museums: generally 9:30am–5pm, closed Monday. Ayasofya 9:30am–5pm, closed Monday. Topkapı 9:30am–5pm daily, closed Tuesday in winter (Harem 10am–4pm). Dolmabahçe Palace 9am–4pm daily (3pm October to February).

Post Offices: main offices 8am-midnight Monday to Saturday, and 9am–7pm on Sundays.

Shops: generally 9:30am–7pm Monday to Saturday, closed noon or 1–2pm, though many tourist shops stay open later and on Sunday. Grand Bazaar, 8am–7pm Monday to Saturday.

PHOTOGRAPHY *(fotoğrafçılık)*

Major brands of film are widely available, but are more expensive than at home. Photo shops in Istanbul and the major resorts can process your colour prints in 24 to 48 hours at reasonable prices, and some provide a 1-hour service. Protect your film from the effects of heat, and never leave a camera or film lying in direct sunlight. The use of flash or tripod is forbidden in many museums, so always check before snapping away. Taking pictures of military subjects and active archaeological excavations is forbidden. If you want to take photographs of the local people avoid causing offence by asking permission first— some country people, especially women, may object.

POLICE *(Polis)* (See also EMERGENCIES)

Turkey's civil police wear green uniforms and are known as the *Polis*. There is a police station *(karakol)* in every city and large town. In the countryside, police duties are carried out by army personnel, called the *Jandarma*: they have khaki military uniforms with a red armband. To telephone the police in an emergency, dial **155.** The *Trafik Polisi* patrol the highways, and man traffic checkpoints (see DRIVING in ISTANBUL on page 112).

Where is the nearest police   **En yakın karakol nerede?**
    station?

PUBLIC HOLIDAYS *(milli bayramlar)*

There are two kinds of public holiday in Turkey— secular holidays, which occur on the same date each year, and religious holidays, which are calculated by the Islamic authorities according to the lunar calendar, and thus occur about 11 days earlier each year. Banks, post offices, government offices and many other businesses will be closed on the following secular holidays:

1 January	*Yılbaşı:* New Year's Day
23 April	*Ulusal Egemenlik ve Çocuk Bayramı:* National Sovereignty and Children's Day (anniversary of first meeting of Republican parliament in Ankara in 1920)

Istanbul

19 May	*Gençlik ve Spor Günü:* Youth and Sports Day (Atatürk's Birthday)
30 August	*Zafer Bayramı:* Victory Day (commemorates conquering of Greeks during the War of Independence in 1922)
29 October	*Cumhuriyet Bayramı:* Republic Day (anniversary of proclamation of the republic by Atatürk in 1923)

There are two national religious holidays, marked by three and four days off respectively. Seaside accommodation and public transport will be booked solid then, and it will be almost impossible to change money. The dates given are the approximate dates for 2000; these fall about 11 days earlier with each succeeding year:

beginning January	*Şeker Bayramı:* "Sugar Festival," the end of the month of Ramadan
mid-January	*Kurban Bayramı:* "Feast of the Sacrifice," commemorating the sacrifice of Abraham

The holy month of Ramadan, during which devout Muslims fast from sunrise to sunset, occupies the four weeks preceding *Šeker Bayramı.* (See also FESTIVALS)

Are you open tomorrow? **Yarın açık mısınız?**

R

RELIGION

The national religion is Islam. Istanbul also supports Christian and Jewish minorities, and there are a number of synagogues and churches in the city. Details of local religious services can be obtained from the tourist office (see also TOURIST INFORMATION OFFICES).

T

TIME DIFFERENCES

Turkish time is GMT plus 2 hours in winter and GMT plus 3 hours in summer, making it 2 hours ahead of the U.K. for most of the year. Turkish clocks go forward on the last Sunday in March, and back on the last Sunday in September; from then until U.K. clocks go back on the last Sunday in October, Turkey is only 1 hour ahead of GMT. The table shows the time difference in various cities in **summer.**

New York	London	**Turkey**	Sydney	Los Angeles
5am	10am	**noon**	8pm	2am

What time is it?   **Saat kaç?**

TIPPING

In a restaurant, it is normal to tip around 10%, even if the bill says that service is included (*servis dahildir*). Hotel porters who carry your bag to your room (this only happens in hotels of 3-stars and up) should get around 75¢ (50p). Taxi drivers don't usually expect a tip, except on the airport route, though it is usual to round up the fare slightly. *Dolmuş* drivers never expect a tip. Gratuities of around 15-20% are looked for in barber shops and Turkish baths, and a few coins, worth around 10p, should be left for the attendant in public toilets.

TOILETS/RESTROOMS *(tuvalet)*

Public toilets are rare, but can usually be found in museums and tourist attractions, and near mosques. They are occasionally of the hole-in-the-floor variety, and sometimes lack toilet paper, so it is a good idea to always carry some with you. *Kadınlar* or *Bayanlar* (Ladies) and *Erkekler* or *Baylar* (Gentlemen).

Where are the toilets/restrooms?   **Tuvaletler nerede?**

Istanbul

TOURIST INFORMATION OFFICES
(Turizm Danışma Bürosu)

The Turkish Ministry of Tourism has branches throughout the country, but outside Istanbul and the main resorts they rarely have much information. The main offices are listed below:

Istanbul: Meşrutiyet Caddesi 57, Tepebaşı, Beyoğlu; tel. (212) 243-3731 or 243-2928. Open 9am–5pm Monday to Friday. There are smaller offices on Divan Yolu in Sultanahmet (by the tram stop), and in the lobby of the Hilton Hotel in Taksim.

İzmir: Akdeniz Mah., 1344 Sokak, Alsancak; tel. (232) 422-1022. Open daily 8:30am–7pm (5pm in winter).

Kuşadası: Liman Caddesi (on the corner opposite entrance to ferry and cruise ship terminal); tel. (256) 614-1103. Open daily 8am–6pm (to 8pm July and August).

Bodrum: Baris Meydanı (on quayside below St Peter's Castle); tel. (252) 316-1091. Open 8am–8pm Monday to Friday, 9am–7:30pm Saturday, closed Sunday.

Their opening hours are generally 8:30am–12:30pm, and 1:30–5:30pm, closed Saturday and Sunday; branches in major tourist areas stay open longer, including weekends. Most towns also have an information office run by the local authorities.

The Ministry of Tourism overseas offices are:

U.K.: 170-173 Piccadilly, London W1V 9DD; tel. (0171) 629-7771 or 355-4207.

U.S.A.: 821 UN Plaza, New York NY 10017; tel. (212) 687-2194.

Where is the tourist office?   **Turizim bürosu nerede?**

TRANSPORT

Buses. Istanbul's bus (*otobus*) service is cheap and frequent, but often slow and crowded. You can buy tickets in booklets of 5 or 10 from the kiosks (*gişe*) at main bus terminals, or from newsstands—look for a sign saying "IETT bilet." One ticket, *bir* or *tek bilet*, is sufficient for most routes; the longer routes require two, *iki* or *çift bilet*.

Dolmuş. A *dolmuş* is basically a shared taxi — a large saloon car or minibus that shuttles back and forth along a set route for a fixed fare. The departure and destination are shown on a sign in the windscreen. The driver waits at the departure point until all the seats are taken, then drops you off wherever you want along the way (*dolmuş* stops are marked by a sign with a "D"). In Istanbul, many *dolmuşes* are beautifully preserved American cars of 1950s vintage.

Ferries. The main point of departure for Istanbul's ferries is Eminönü, between Sirkeci railway station and the Galata Bridge. The jetty nearest the bridge is marked *3 Boğaz Hattı* (Bosphorus Lines), for trips along the Bosphorus; next are the *2 Üsküdar* and *1 Kadıköy* jetties, for boats across to the Asian side; then comes the car ferry to Harem, near Haydarpaşa railway station, also on the Asian side; and finally, off to the right through a gate, is the Adalar (Princes' Islands) jetty. For all ferries, before departure, buy a ticket or *jeton* from the ticket desk (*gişe*) where prices and timetables are displayed.

There are also ferries along the Golden Horn, which depart from jetties near the large Chamber of Commerce building.

Taxis. Istanbul taxis are bright yellow. They can be hailed in the street, picked up at a rank, or ordered by telephone from your hotel. All taxis have meters and are required by law to use them. Most drivers are honest, but a few may try to rip you off, especially on the trip from the airport to the city centre; if you want to pay in foreign currency, you will probably be charged more than the going rate. Note that fares increase by 50% between midnight and 6am. If you take a taxi across the Bosphorus Bridge, you will have to pay the bridge toll on top of the fare. Few drivers speak English, so it's worth writing down your destination on a piece of paper.

Trains. There is a suburban rail service which runs from Sirkeci westwards along the coast to Yeşilköy. For the visitor, it is only of use for getting to Yedikule and Ataköy. Buy a flat-rate *banliyö* (sub-urban) ticket on the platform, and keep it until the end of the journey.

Trams. Istanbul has a new light rail service (*tramvay*) which runs from Sirkeci out to the Topkapı bus station at the city walls, and on into the suburbs. The section of line between Aksaray and Sirkeci stops at Sultanahmet (Ayasofya, Topkapı and the Blue Mosque), Çemberlitaş (Grand Bazaar) and Laleli (hotels). You must buy a ticket (*bilet*) from a booth near the tram stop. Trams run every 5 minutes or so. A restored 19th-century tram runs along İstiklal Caddesi, from the top station of the Tünel to Taksim Square.

Tünel. Istanbul's tiny underground train, the Tünel, climbs the steep hill from the Galata Bridge up to Pera. To get to the bottom station, bear right from the bridge and enter a pedestrian underpass full of shops; at its far end, go up the left-hand stairs, and head for the news-stand straight ahead. The rather inconspicuous entrance is first on the right by the news-stand. Buy a tiny token (*jeton*) and place it in the turnstile slot. Trains leave every few minutes, and take only 90 seconds to reach the top. (A new metro system is being built in Istanbul, but the network is designed more for commuters than tourists.)

Where's the nearest bus/ dolmuş stop?	**En yakın otobüs/ dolmuş durağı nerededir?**
When's the next ferry/bus train to…?	**…bir sonra ki vapur/otobüs tren saat kaçta?**
I want a ticket to…	**…'(a) bir bilet istiyorum.**
single (one-way)	**gidiş**
return (round-trip)	**gidiş-dönüş**
first/second class	**birinci/ikinci mevki**
What's the fare to…?	**…için ücret nedir?**
Will you tell me when to get off?	**Ne zaman inmem gerektiğini söyler misiniz?**

TRAVELLERS with DISABILITIES

There are very few facilities for travellers with disabilities in Turkey, even the new light rail service (see opposite) is not wheelchair-accessible. Some of the more modern (and expensive) hotels, however, do have wheelchair access. Check wit your travel agent for information on hotels that offer facilities for travellers with disabilities.

TRAVELLING TO TURKEY

By Air

Scheduled flights

From the U.K.: The national airline, THY (*Türk Hava Yolları* — Turkish Airlines), flies twice daily from London Heathrow to Istanbul, and twice weekly to İzmir, with connecting services to cities throughout Turkey. For details tel. (0171) 499-4499. British Airways also offers two flights a day from Heathrow to Istanbul. For details, contact British Airways, tel. (0345) 222 111 (London Area) or (01345) 222111 (rest of U.K.).

From the U.S.A. and Canada: Turkish Airlines has regular non-stop flights from New York, Chicago, and Los Angeles to Istanbul. For details, tel. (212) 339-9650. Delta Airlines also flies non-stop from New York to Istanbul.

Charter flights and package tours

From the U.K. and Ireland: Available from Dublin, Gatwick, Manchester, Glasgow, and a number of other British cities to İzmir and Dalaman (on the south coast near Marmaris). These are available as flight only (cheaper than a scheduled flight, but with more restrictions), or as part of a hotel or self-catering package holiday. Most companies offer the choice of a two-centre holiday combining Istanbul and a coastal resort such as Kuşadası or Bodrum.

From the U.S.A. and Canada: There are no charter flights from North America to Turkey. Your best bet is to go via the U.K. or Europe.

Istanbul

By Road

From the U.K., the main overland route to Turkey passes through Germany, Austria, Hungary, Romania and Bulgaria. You will need transit visas for Romania and Bulgaria; apply to the appropriate consulates at least 10 days in advance. The distance from London to Istanbul is about 3,000 km (1,870 miles) for which you should allow at least four days of steady driving.

Driving time can be cut by heading to Italy and using the summer car-ferry services from Venice to İzmir, or from Ancona to Kuşadası. Reservations must be made well in advance.

By Rail

Transit visas are required for Romania and Bulgaria. Allow about three days for the full journey from London to Istanbul. For details, contact British Rail at London Victoria, tel. (071) 834-2345.

The *Inter-Rail Card*, permitting 30 days of unlimited travel in certain European countries to people under 26, is also valid for Turkey.

W

WATER

Tap water is considered to be unsafe, and you are advised to avoid drinking it. Bottled mineral water is easily obtainable everywhere.

I'd like a bottle of mineral water.	**Bir şişe maden suyu istiyorum.**
carbonated/still	**soda/su**

WOMEN TRAVELLERS

Foreign women travelling in Turkey are occasionally subject to harassment from local men. Many Turkish men have the idea that European women are "easy." A woman accompanied by a man is less likely to attract unwanted attention, but is not immune.

The best strategy is to dress modestly, with long trousers, or a long skirt, and a long-sleeved, loose-fitting top.

Recommended Hotels

Finding accommodation in Istanbul is rarely a problem, as the city has recently seen a boom in the hotel business. However, if you want a room in a particular hotel, it is best to book, especially during July and August. The main hotel areas are Laleli, Aksaray, and Sultanahmet in the Old City, and around Taksim Square in Beyoğlu. Intense competition among the middle-range hotels means that you can often bargain for a lower rate, especially if you plan to stay for more than two nights.

As a basic guide we have used the symbols below to indicate prices for a double room with bath, including breakfast:

✪✪✪✪✪	over £130 ($200)
✪✪✪✪	£80–130 ($120-200)
✪✪✪	£50–80 ($75-120)
✪✪	£30–50 ($45-75)
✪	below £30 ($45

STAMBOUL (OLD CITY)

Alzer ✪✪✪ *At Meydanı 72, Sultanahmet; Tel. (212) 516-6262, fax (212) 516-0000.* Comfortable and conveniently situated across from the Blue Mosque. Bowls of fresh cherries in your room. Noise from muezzin at dawn in front rooms. 18 rooms.

And ✪✪✪ *Yerebatan Caddesi, Camii Sokak 46, Sultanahmet; Tel. (212) 512-0207, fax (212) 512-3025.* An unassuming hotel located in a back street opposite Yerebatan Sarayı. All rooms are *en suite* with private bath and satellite TV and most have magnificent views of the Old City. The hotel's rooftop restaurant offers a panoramic view of Haghia Sophia and the Bosphorus. 45 rooms.

Istanbul

Ayasofya Pensions ✣✣✣✣ *Soğukçeşme Sokak, Sultanahmet; Tel. (212) 513-3660, fax (212) 513-3669.* Beautifully restored wooden Ottoman houses in quiet back street right beside entrance to Topkapı Palace. Rooms have private bath, period furniture, and Turkish carpets. You can eat in nearby Sarnıç Restaurant (see page 139). 57 rooms.

Four Seasons Hotel ✣✣✣✣ *Tevfikhane Sokak 1, Sultanhamet; Tel. (212) 638-8200, fax (212) 638-8210.* The city's newest luxury hotel, and some say its best, occupies a former prison near the Topkapı Palace and Blue Mosque. Large, antiques- and kilm-filled rooms overlook a courtyard. Excellent restaurant. 65 rooms.

Grand Lord ✣-✣✣ *Mesipaşa Mahallesi, Azimkar Sokak 22-24, Laleli; Tel. (212) 518-6311, fax (212) 518-6400.* This is a good value-for-money hotel in a convenient location. The small but comfortable rooms all have a TV and private shower. Staff are friendly and always eager to be of service. 42 rooms.

Hotel Empress Zoe ✣✣ *Akbiyik Cadessi, Adirye Sokak 10, Sultanhamet; Tel. (212) 518-4360, fax (212) 518-5699.* A small, intimate hotel with nicely decorated rooms filled with antiques and textiles. 12 rooms.

Ibrahim Pasa Oteli ✣✣✣ *Terzihane Sokak 5, Sultanhamet; Tel. (212) 518-0395, fax (212) 518-4457.* A wonderfully restored Ottoman house, with exquisitely decorated rooms, some affording views of the Bosphorous, Restaurant, bar, rooftop terrace. 19 rooms.

Kalyon Hotel ✣✣✣ *Sahil Yolu, Sultanhamet; Tel. (212) 517-4400, fax (212) 638-1111.* Nicely located on the shore road beneath the Blue Mosque, overlooking the Sea of Marmara and within walking distance of Topkapı Palace and other

Sultanhamet sights. Nice views of mosques or harbour from rooms, seaside garden and restaurant. 110 rooms.

Kariye ❀❀-❀❀❀ *Kariye Camii Sokak 18, Edirnekapı; Tel. (212) 534-8414, fax (212) 521-6631.* Beautifully restored, pastel green wooden mansion next door to the Byzantine mosaics of Kariye Museum. There is a pleasant garden restaurant and bar. Very peaceful location, about 10 minutes' taxi ride from Sultanahmet. 27 rooms.

Küçük Ayasofya ❀-❀❀ *Şehit Mehmet Paşa Sokak 25, Sultanahmet; Tel. (212) 516-1988, fax (212) 516-8356.* Small, friendly hotel in restored 19th-century wooden house located near the Blue Mosque. All rooms are *en suite* with private shower and toilet, telephone and central heating. 14 rooms.

Merit Antique ❀❀❀❀ *Ordu Caddesi 226, Laleli; Tel. (212) 513-9300, (212) 513-9340 for reservations, fax (212) 512-6390.* (Formerly the Ramada.) Built in the 1920s, this hotel, with its attractive mix of modern trimmings and original architecture, comprises four buildings around glass-roofed atriums. Indoor pool, sauna and jacuzzi. 287 rooms.

Park ❀ *Utangaç Sokak 26, Sultanahmet; Tel. (212) 517-6596, fax (212) 518-9602.* This budget hotel has modern rooms all with private shower and is in a good location downhill from the Blue Mosque towards the sea. Roof terrace with view of Sea of Marmara. 27 rooms.

President ❀❀❀❀ *Tiyatro Caddesi 25, Beyazıt; Tel. (212) 516-6980, fax (212) 516-6999.* Part of Best Western International chain. The rooms are comfortable, *en suite* with private bath, satellite TV, and minibar. There is an indoor swimming pool and sun-deck. 204 rooms.

Yeşil Ev ✿✿✿✿ *Kabasakal Caddesi 5, Sultanahmet; Tel. (212) 517-6785, fax (212) 517-6780*. One of Istanbul's most famous and popular hotels, set in a restored, four-storey wooden mansion behind the Blue Mosque. Rooms have Ottoman brass beds and period furniture. Beautiful garden restaurant. 20 rooms.

BEYOGLU (NEW CITY)

Büyük Londra ✿✿ *Meşrutiyet Caddesi 117, Tepebaşı; Tel. (212) 245-0670, fax (212) 245-0671*. A fine old building uphill from the Pera Palas, and much cheaper. All rooms have private bath, and many have a balcony overlooking Golden Horn. Decorated in 19th-century Ottoman style. 54 rooms.

Conrad International Istanbul ✿✿✿✿ *Barbaros Bul. 46, Besiktas; Tel. (212) 227-3000, fax (212) 259-6667*. One of Istanbul's largest hotels is noted for its unusually comfortable rooms, furnished in contemporary Italian style and affording extensive views over the city. Indoor pool, outdoor pool, tennis courts, extensive gardens, two restaurants, three bars. 627 rooms.

Dilson ✿✿✿ *Sıraselviler Caddesi 49, Taksim; Tel. (212) 252-9600, fax (212) 249-7077*. An attractive modern hotel situated near Taksim Square. All the rooms are *en suite* with private bath, air-conditioning, and satellite TV. 111 rooms.

Divan ✿✿✿ *Cumhuriyet Cadessi 2, Sisli; Tel. (212) 248-8527, fax (212) 8527*. A modern hotel near Taksim, with large, comfortable rooms and excellent service. Noted for its restaurant serving traditional Turkish dishes (see page 139). 180 rooms.

Family House ✿✿-✿✿✿ *Gümüşsuyu Kutlu Sokak 53, Taksim; Tel. (212) 249-7351, fax (212) 249-9667*. An "apart-hotel" with 5 apartments. Each has 2 bedrooms (1 double, 1 twin), living room, a kitchen, bathroom, and TV. Laundry and baby-sitting service. Ideal for families.

Istanbul Hilton ❀❀❀❀ *Cumhuriyet Caddesi, Harbiye; Tel. (212) 231-4646, fax (212) 240-4165.* This huge, luxury hotel complex near Taksim Square is ideal for sports enthusiasts. It has 3 swimming pools, tennis, and squash courts. All rooms have private bath, satellite TV and air-conditioning. 498 rooms.

Pera Palas ❀❀❀❀ *Meşrutiyet Caddesi 98-100, Tepebaşı; Tel. (212) 251-4560, fax (212) 251-4088.* The city's oldest hotel built 1892 for Orient Express passengers. Grandiose lobby and bar, beautifully renovated rooms with period atmosphere, all the modern facilities you could wish for. 3 restaurants, 2 pâtisseries. 149 rooms.

Richmond ❀❀❀❀ *İstiklal Caddesi 445, Beyoğlu; Tel. (212) 252-5460, fax (212) 252-9707.* Short walk from Tünel top station. Air-conditioned rooms with bath and satellite TV. 107 rooms.

Star ❀❀ *İnönü Caddesi, Sağlık Sokak 11-13, Gümüşsuyu; Tel. (212) 293-1860, fax (212) 251-7822.* Rooms are small but comfortable, with private shower. Off Taksim Square. 26 rooms.

Swissotel The Bosphorous ❀❀❀❀ *Cadessi 2, Macka; Tel. (212) 259-0101, fax (212) 259-0150.* One of the most pleasant of the modern international-style hotels that have gone up around Taksim Square. Views of the Bosphorous, and within walking distance to Dolmabahçe Palace. Turkish bath, indoor and outdoor swimming pools, nine restaurants. 500 rooms, 100 suites.

Yenişehir Palas ❀❀-❀❀❀ *Meşrutiyet Caddesi, Oteller Sokak 1-3, Tepebaşı; Tel. (212) 249-8810, fax (212) 249-7507.* Central Beyoğlu location. All rooms with bath, satellite TV, and air-conditioning. 134 rooms.

THE BOSPHORUS AND
THE SEA OF MARMARA

Bebek ✿✿-✿✿✿ *CevdetPaşa Caddesi 113-115, Bebek; Tel. (212) 263-3000, fax (212) 263-2636.* A small, old-fashioned hotel in the middle of the lovely suburb of Bebek, about 10 km (6¼ miles) from the city centre. The rooms at the back enjoy a fine view over the Bosphorus. 27 rooms.

Çırağan Palace ✿✿✿✿✿ *Çırağan Caddesi 84, Beşiktaş; Tel. (212) 258-3377, fax (212) 259-6687.* A new luxury hotel in a restored 19th-century Ottoman palace that graces the shores of the Bosphorus. Hotel boasts a health club, a sauna, Turkish bath, shopping centre, plus indoor and outdoor pools. 324 rooms.

Epos ✿✿ *Istanbul Caddesi, Havlucular Sokak 3, Bakırköy; Tel. (212) 561-1650, fax (212) 571-6437.* Comfortable and welcoming hotel above the coast road near Galleria. All rooms have private shower and air-conditioning. Only 10 minutes by taxi from the airport. 37 rooms.

Holiday Inn Crown Plaza ✿✿✿✿ *Sahil Yolu, Ataköy; Tel. (212) 560-4110, fax (212) 559-4905.* A luxury hotel overlooking Ataköy Marina and the Galleria shopping centre, only 8 km (5 miles) from the airport. Fitness centre, conference rooms. 170 rooms.

PRINCES' ISLANDS

Hotel Merit Halki Palace ✿✿✿ *Refah Sehitleri Cadessi 88, Heybeliada; Tel. (216) 351-9550, fax (216) 351-8483.* A beautiful Ottoman villa converted to a hotel, with flower filled terraces and large gardens. Swimming pool. Only 30 minutes from the center of Istanbul by boat, and a pleasant place to stay when visiting the city in summer. 45 rooms.

Splendid Palace ✹✹✹ *Buyuk Ada; Tel. (216) 382-6950.* An Art Nouveau gem that has been beautifully restored, offering guests a special retreat on the largest of the Princes' Islands. Beautiful, antiques-filled rooms, swimming pools, gardens. 70 rooms, four suites.

FROM ISTANBUL

If you plan to take a trip out of Istanbul proper, below are a few suggestions of some hotels in the surrounding areas where you can spend one or several nights.

BODRUM

Manastır ✹✹✹ *Barış Sitesi Mevkii, Kumbahçe Mahallesi; Tel. (252) 316-2854, fax (252) 316-2772.* Ultra-civilized hotel aloof on the hillside above Bodrum's centre. Great views from terraced bar; restaurant and pool. 51 air-conditioned rooms.

Parkım Palas ✹✹ *Gümbet; Tel. (252) 316-1504, fax (252) 316-3865.* Good package hotel right on the beach. A big pool and 99 rooms in low-rise blocks in a garden full of bananas and bougainvillaea. Half-board compulsory.

Seçkin Konaklar ✹-✹✹ *Neyzen Tevfik Caddesi 246; Tel. (252) 316-1351, fax (252) 316-3336.* Whitewashed low-rise accommodation blocks used by tour operators. The blocks surround a pleasant pool and are situated at the quiet end of town behind the marina. 48 rooms.

Taşkule ✹✹ *Yalıkavak; Tel. and fax (252) 385-4935.* B&B used by British tour operator, on the water's edge. There are 11 exceptionally pretty rooms, each with sofa, fresh flowers, and swanky bathroom, as well as a pool and bar.

BURSA

Safran ❀❀❀ *Kale Sokak 4; Tel. (224) 224-7216, fax (224) 224-7219.* A restored Ottoman mansion behind the Citadel; air-conditioned rooms, excellent restaurant. 10 rooms.

IZMIR

Karaca ❀❀ *Necatibey Bulvari 1379, Sok. 55; Tel. (232) 489-1940, fax (232) 483-1498.* On a quiet street near the city's bazaar. Rooms are air-conditioned and many have balconies. 73 rooms.

KUSADASI

Kismet ❀❀❀❀ *Akyar Mevkii; Tel. (256) 614-2005, fax (256) 614-4914.* One of Turkey's most enjoyable and famous hotels is stunningly situated on a seaside peninsula at the edge of town, surrounded by lush gardens. Guests have included Queen Elizabeth II and former U.S. President Jimmy Carter. The large rooms all have terraces and face either the harbour or the open sea. Restaurant, bar, beach. 107 rooms.

PAMUKKALE

Kervansaray ❀❀❀ *Inonu Cadessi; Tel. (258) 272-2209.* A charming pension in the village centre, just below the terraces. Rooftop restaurant, swimming pool. Very friendly service. 14 rooms.

Koru ❀❀ *Pamukkale; Tel. (258) 272-2429, fax (258) 272-2023.* The best hotel up on the terraces, with four pools (one indoor) and majestic views. The Koru has 132 air-conditioned rooms. Due to plans to protect Pamukkale, this hotel may be closing, so check in advance.

Recommended Restaurants

Istanbul offers a wide range of eating places, from cheap kebab stalls to expensive hotel restaurants. The inexpensive *kebapcis* and *köftecis* in the backstreets of Sultanahmet and Laleli often serve up far tastier meals than the tourist traps, and at half the price. At the other end of the scale, you get what you pay for—exquisitely prepared Ottoman cuisine in the top hotel restaurants, or the freshest of seafood in one of the many restaurants along the shores of the Bosphorus.

Below is a list of restaurants recommended by Berlitz; if you find other places you think are worth recommending, we'd be pleased to hear from you.

As a basic guide we have used the following symbols to give you some idea of what you can expect to pay for a three-course meal for two, excluding drinks:

✿✿✿	over £30 ($45)
✿✿✿	£15–30 ($20–45)
✿	below £15 ($20)

STAMBOUL (OLD CITY)

Firat ✿ *Cakmaktas Sokak 11, Kumpaki; Tel. (212) 517-2308.* This restaurant is just one of the 50 or so seafood establishments that are packed into a few narrow streets near the old fishing docks at the southern end of the Stamboul peninsula. Firat is one of the nicer places to dine, and is noted for the quality of its fresh fish dishes, many of which are baked according to old Ottoman recipes.

Istanbul

Hamdi Et Lokantasi ❀ *Kalcin Sokak, Eminonu; Tel. (212) 528-0390.* A simple, unpretentious restaurant specializing in grilled meat dishes. Open for lunch only; no alcohol is served.

Havuzlu ❀-❀❀ *Gani Çelebi Sokak 3, Kapalı Çarşı; Tel. 527-3346.* Traditional Turkish cuisine in the heart of the Grand Bazaar. Open for lunch only. Closed Sunday.

Konyali ❀❀❀ *Topkapı Palace; Tel.(212) 513-9696.* A surprisingly good restaurant, specializing in Turkish cuisine, in a splendid setting: a courtyard of the Topkapı Palace, with enchanting views over the Bosphorous. Open for lunch only; closed Tuesday.

Lale ❀❀❀ *Merit Antique Hotel, Ordu Caddesi 226, Laleli; Tel. 513-9300 ext. 5054.* Serves top quality Turkish cuisine. The hotel also has an excellent Chinese. Booking recommended.

Ocakbaşı ❀❀-❀❀❀ *President Hotel, Tiyatro Caddesi 25, Beyazıt; Tel. 516-6980.* Offers international and Turkish cuisine. Buffet lunch noon to 3pm. There is folk music and belly-dancing in the evening. Hotel also has an English-style pub.

Pandeli's ❀❀ *Mısır Çarşısı 51, Eminönü; Tel. 527-3009.* Above the main entrance to Spice Bazaar, famed for excellent food. Open for lunch only. Closed Sunday and holidays.

Pudding Shop ❀ *Divan Yolu 18, Sultanahmet. No telephone.* Famous backpackers' haunt of the 1960s and 1970s. Turkish-style self-service cafeteria, with excellent puddings such as *fırın sütlaç* (baked rice pudding).

Rami ❀❀-❀❀❀ *Utangaç Sokak 6, Sultanahmet; Tel. 517-6593.* Romantic, candle-lit restaurant set in a restored wooden mansion with period furniture. Located on the far side of the Blue Mosque from the Hippodrome. Seafood and Turkish dishes.

Sarnıç ✹✹ *Soğukçeşme Sokak, Sultanahmet; Tel. 512-4291.* Atmospheric restaurant set amid the vaults and pillars of a 1,000 year-old Byzantine cistern. A huge, open fireplace makes this a cosy dinner spot during winter. International menu with a few Turkish specialities.

Yeşil Ev Hotel ✹✹ *Kabasakal Caddesi 5, Sultanahmet; Tel. 517-6785.* This fine old Ottoman mansion has a restaurant set in its cool, shady garden, with tables set around a tinkling fountain. Offers a choice of traditional Turkish or more international dishes.

BEYOGLU (NEW CITY)

Asir ✹✹ *Kalyoncu Kulluk Cadessi 94/1, Beyoglu; Tel. (212) 250-0557.* Wonderful selection of *meze* (appetizers) and fish dishes make this a popular spot for visitors and locals alike.

Çatı ✹✹ *İstiklal Caddesi, Orhan A. Apaydın Sokak 20-27, Beyoğlu; Tel. 251-0000.* Pleasant rooftop restaurant (on the seventh floor) and popular with locals. Interesting menu of Turkish and international dishes, including unusual Ottoman desserts such as candied tomato with walnut. Closed on Sundays.

Çiçek Pasajı ✹ *İstiklal Caddesi, Galatasaray.* Not one restaurant, but several, grouped together along this 19th-century arcade. Popular with tourists and locals, you can enjoy a full meal, or just a snack of fried mussels and chips and wash it down with a beer.

Divan ✹✹ *Divan Hotel, Cumhuriyet Cad. 2, Beyoglu, Taksim; Tel. (212) 231-4100.* For many travellers this is the best place in

Istanbul to enjoy genuine Turkish cooking. The 21-item *meze* (appetizer) platter constitutes a meal in itself.

Dört Mevsim ✸✸ *İstiklal Caddesi 509, Tünel; Tel. 293-3941.* Attractive restaurant in unassuming brick-fronted building near Tünel top station. Nineteenth-century furnishings, fine Turkish and international cuisine.

Galata Kulesi ✸✸ *Büyük Hendek Caddesi, Şişhane; Tel. 245-1160.* Enjoy the fine views from this restaurant set at the top of the Galata Tower. Turkish, French and international cuisine, with live music in the evenings.

Hacibaba ✸✸ *İstiklal Caddesi 49, Beyoglu; Tel. (212) 244-1886.* Typical Turkish restaurant with charm and a large selection of Turkish specialties. There is seating on the pretty terrace in good weather.

Rejans ✸✸ *Emir Navraz Sokak 15, Galatasaray; Tel. 244-1610.* This famous restaurant was founded in the 1930s by White Russians fleeing the effects of the Russian Revolution. Excellent menu includes classics such as borscht and chicken Kiev. Closed Sunday.

Revan ✸✸✸ *Sheraton Hotel, Taksim Parkı; Tel. 231-2121.* Luxury rooftop restaurant specializing in Ottoman cuisine. If the menu is too intimidating, you can opt for the ten-course set dinner, at a reasonable price.

BOSPHORUS

Beyti ✸✸ *Ormon Sokak 8, Florya; Tel. (212) 663-2990.* An Istanbul institution famous for its grilled meats, most notably the skewered lamb filets known as Beyti kabob. Weather permitting, meals are served in a charming garden. Near the airport; best reached from the city centre by taxi.

Café Çamlıca ❋❋ *Büyük Çamlıca Parkı, Ümraniye; Tel. (216) 335-3301.* Beautiful setting in hilltop park above Üsküdar, the highest point in Istanbul, with wonderful view over the Bosphorus to the minarets of Stamboul and, on a clear day, southwest to the snow-capped Uludağ (Great Mountain). Serves standard Turkish fare.

Cafe du Levant ❋❋ *Haskoy Cadessi 27, Sutluce.* A popular spot serving excellent French bistro food; wonderful views over the Golden Horn.

Kaptan ❋❋ *Birinci Caddesi 53, Arnavutköy; Tel. 265-8487.* Former fisherman's restaurant on the shores of the strait that is now a popular eating place for the local students and ex-patriates. Offers a wide selection of fresh fish that are prepared practically straight from the net.

Kizkulesi Deniz ❋❋ *Salacak Sahil Yolu 41, Uskudar; Tel (216) 341-0403.* One of the most popular fish restaurants in Istanbul, Kizkulesi Deniz is on the Asian side of the river, and affords stunning views over the Bosphorous and Istanbul's striking skyline.

Körfez ❋❋❋ *Körfez Caddesi 78, Kanlıca; Tel. (216) 322-0108.* This superlative seafood restaurant is situated on the Asian side of the Bosphorus. If you call in advance, the owner will organize a personal ride on his boat that will ferry you across the strait. The house speciality is *levrek tuzda* (sea bass baked in salt). Closed Monday.

Istanbul

Memo's ✸✸ *Salhane Sokak 10/2, Ortakoy; Tel. (212) 261-8304.* A chic bar and restaurant that is always popular with young professionals, especially so in summer, when a waterside terrace is open. A disco on the premises begins hopping after midnight.

Mey ✸✸✸ *Rumeli Hisari Cadessi, Bebeki Apt. 122, Bebek; Tel. (212) 265-2599.* An excellent fish restaurant, with chic decor and a crowd to match. Reservations essential.

Resat Pasa Konagi ✸✸ *Sinan Ercan Cadessi 34/1, Kozyatagi Mah., Erenkoy; Tel. (216) 361-3411.* A very popular eatery in an old villa on the Asian side. The Pasa Sofrasi, a tasting menu, allows you to enjoy an excellent selection of *meze* (appetizers) and kebabs, accompanied by excellent Turkish wines.

Tu'ra ✸✸✸ *Çırağan Palace Hotel, Çırağan Caddesi 84, Beşiktaş; Tel. 258-3377.* One of the city's newest restaurants and definitely one of its most luxurious, set in the sumptuous surroundings of a restored imperial palace (the name of the restaurant is Turkish for the sultan's monogram). The Tu'ra offers a diverse menu of rich and interesting Ottoman cuisine. Closed Monday.

FROM ISTANBUL

BODRUM

Han ✸✸ *Kale Caddesi 23; Tel. 316-7951.* An 18th-century caravanserai with a range of international and Turkish cuisine that is served in a lovely candlelit courtyard. There is belly dancing offered for entertainment throughout the evening.

Kocadon ✸✸ *Neyzen Tevfik Caddesi 160.* The most stylish setting of the many restaurants behind the marina—an artfully lit courtyard between two old stone buildings. Beautiful displays of help-yourself *meze*.

Restaurant Alley ❀❀ *Off Kale Caddesi.* Usually a party atmosphere in this very pretty, vine-covered lane crammed to bursting with simple, traditional Turkish restaurants.

BURSA

Adanur Kebapci ❀ *Unlu Cadessi, Heykel.* A good place to sample the local specialty, a lamb dish known as Iskender Kebap.

CESME

Sahil ❀ *Cumhuriyet Meydanı.* A large, dynamic fish restaurant on the main square, popular with tourists and locals alike. Complimentary post-prandial liqueur.

IZMIR

Deniz ❀❀❀ *İzmir Palas Hotel, Vasif Cinar Bulvari 2; Tel. (232) 422-0601.* An elegant waterfront restaurant known best for its fresh fish.

KUSADASI

Club Caravanserai ❀❀❀ *Atatürk Bulvarı 1; Tel. 614-4115.* Ottoman caravanserai now a (very noisy) hotel and restaurant with a candlelit, palmy courtyard for nightly dinner cabaret shows (belly dancing etc.).

Sultan Han ❀❀ *Bahar Sokak 8; Tel. 614-6380.* A superb, broad-beamed old mansion in the Kale district with outdoor dining in a lovely viney courtyard and nightly belly dancing. Extensive *meze*.

ABOUT BERLITZ

In 1878 Professor Maximilian Berlitz had a revolutionary idea about making language learning accessible and enjoyable. One hundred and twenty years later these same principles are still successfully at work.

For language instruction, translation and inter-pretation services, cross-cultural training, study abroad programs, and an array of publishing products and additional services, visit any one of our more than 350 Berlitz Centers in over 40 countries.

Please consult your local telephone directory for the Berlitz Center nearest you or visit our web site at http://www.berlitz.com.

Helping the World Communicate